Scrum Fundamentals

A Beginner's Guide to Mastery of The Scrum Project Management Methodology

Jeff Cohn

no scenarios in which the publisher or the original author of this work can be in any fashion deemed liable for any hardship or damages that may befall them after undertaking information described herein.

Additionally, the information in the following pages is intended only for informational purposes and should thus be thought of as universal. As befitting its nature, it is presented without assurance regarding its prolonged validity or interim quality. Trademarks that are mentioned are done without written consent and can in no way be considered an endorsement from the trademark holder.

Table of contents

Introduction

Thank you very much for purchasing, "*Scrum Fundamentals. A beginner's guide to mastery of the Scrum project management methodology.*" It's really exciting to see that you are interested in learning more about Agile methodologies, in particular, Scrum.

If you are new to project management, then you are about to discover a new world filled with many possibilities. Project management is not an easy area to master since many factors come into play when you are embarking upon a new journey such this one.

If you are a veteran of project management, but new to Scrum, then I think you will find an interesting way in which you can improve your current knowledge of project management methodologies and how this book can allow you to find new tools.

If you are familiar with Scrum, then I hope this book can serve you as a refresher, but also help you reflect on how you can build on your existing knowledge of Scrum and the various elements that go into this methodology.

When you begin learning about the Agile world, you begin to uncover the different possibilities that can become unlocked by a simple shift in mindset. Now, one of the most common misconceptions is that one project management methodology is better than another. And that is simply not true.

This isn't a question about which methodology is better. This is about understanding the applications that Agile, in particular, Scrum, have in certain projects as compared to others.

As such, when you think about Agile, think about how your projects may benefit from a methodology that contemplates change and uncertainty as a part of the normal course of the project.

Does that sound familiar?

You see, traditional project management methodologies contemplate a more stable working environment. These methodologies, such as the methodology espoused by the Project Management Institute, are ideal for those environments in which there are much more stable conditions. For instance, think about projects which have already been done many times before.

Therefore, traditional project management methodologies are great for those projects which have set rules and guidelines in place. For instance, road constructions, buildings, social programs are all examples of how traditional project management methodologies can be utilized to achieve the objectives of the stakeholders in the project.

Now, what about those projects which have

tight deadlines, uncertain conditions, and continuous change?

This is where Agile shines.

Of course, most folks think of software development when they think of Agile and Scrum. While this is true, Agile methodologies have grown to such a point where they can be applied to a wide array of fields. In particular, Scrum can be implemented in those fields which have a high degree of uncertainty or when there is a considerable amount of change involved.

Agile is all about making a continuous improvement on a product/service, and how they are being delivered. This is a key difference.

In traditional project management methodologies, the deliverables aren't seen until the end of the project. In the case of Agile, the presentation of deliverables is incremental. What that means is that project stakeholders won't have to wait until the end of the project to see if the deliverables actually work.

With Scrum, the focus is on delivering incremental results so that effectiveness can be measured before the final delivery of the product. This means that Scrum practitioners will have the opportunity to fix things on the fly and not have to wait until after the project has concluded in order to fix any bugs in the final deliverables.

At this point, you might be asking yourself:

what is the difference between Agile and Scrum?

And, that is a fair question.

Agile is a philosophy, an approach, to project management. Agile is based on continuous improvement and a consistent search for improved quality. This led to the development of the Agile Manifesto.

The Agile Manifesto is a document which encompasses the spirit of Agile: getting improved results in the least amount of time possible, with continuous improvement on the quality of outputs.

Since Agile was born out of the software industry, it considers *time* as one of the most valuable resources that team members can learn to cherish and value.

Speaking of valuable resources, Agile methodologies place a high degree of value on *people*.

Unlike other project management approaches in which material resources are more valuable than people, Agile and Scrum place a large amount of focus on people and the role they play within the teams they belong to.

With Agile, a flat, non-hierarchical structure is considered to be the best way in which teams can be productive. The leadership roles played by the Scrum Master and the Product Owner are not to give orders, or even determine what needs to be done.

The roles of these leaders are more of a servant leadership in which they are motivated to provide their team members with everything they need in order to become successful and achieve the objectives set forth at the outset of the project.

As you can see, Scrum places a great deal of value on collaboration and teamwork rather than on "directing" and "guiding." While leaders certainly bear their share of responsibility, responsibility is shared by all members of the team. Therefore, if anything goes wrong, it's the team's collective responsibility. But, if everything goes right, it's the team's collective victory.

This attitude makes Scrum an incredibly collaborative methodology in which all team members are working together to reach the same goal. It should be said that members of a Scrum team should all be on the same page and subscribe to the same beliefs.

As such, this book looks to dig deeper into the elements that make Scrum a great project management methodology in which you, and your organization, can improve their collaborative nature. So, we will be really drilling down on the most important aspects of Scrum, and how you can apply them into your organization right away.

So, buckle up because we are going to be heading for quite a ride. I am sure you will enjoy every bit of it.

Chapter 1: Introduction to Agile and Its Principles

In the first chapter of this book, we are going to be taking a closer look at what Agile is, and its underlying principles. Like any other philosophies, there are concepts, principles, axioms, and tents which guide the activities that are to be conducted under the umbrella of this methodology.

As such, we are going to be drilling down on the definition of Agile, its 12 principles and we are even going to talk a little bit about this history of Agile. So, let's get started.

Defining Agile

Our starting point for this discussion in the definition of Agile. In the introduction, we used the terms "Agile" and "Scrum" rather interchangeably, though they are two completely different concepts.

First of all, Agile is all about adapting to change. It is about being able to adapt and succeed in an uncertain and turbulent environment.

As we stated earlier, Agile methodologies are focused on thriving in situations in which projects don't always have a stable environment.

So, what does it mean to be in an uncertain and turbulent environment?

11

It means that there are lots of questions surrounding your tasks with little to no clarity on stability.

Now, before you panic and head for the door, allow me to elaborate.

In the introduction, I mentioned how there are projects which experts basically have down cold.

Think of construction.

When engineers build a road, they have a clear idea about what specifications are needed to the materials to be used, they are aware of the topography and have a very good idea about the costs associated with the project. Since road construction has been around for a while, there is a great deal of information on how to deal with the potential risks that come with this task.

So, traditional project management methodologies are ideal for this type of task since there are predictable outcomes, predictable inputs, and predictable processes. Sure, there is always the risk for some unforeseen or even fortuitous event which may derail a project, but that's a bit unlikely.

Now, let's consider a technical project, that could be any type of technology and not just software. The uncertainty is born out of the fact that you are producing something that's never been done before or applied in a certain way to the nuances of your project/organization.

Can you see where the uncertainty lies?

In this case, in projects that lead to outcomes which have never produced before, you can't truly anticipate everything that will happen. But you must be prepared to deal with changes as they happen. For instance, you believe that there is a good way of doing something, but as you test the technology, it doesn't run the way you thought it would. So, you need to find another way of making it work properly.

Based on this logic, Scrum is an ideal way for project managers to find a project management methodology which can espouse change without having to resort to complex procedures in order to get all the stakeholders involved to sign off on each move. This makes the process more "Agile" and thereby reduces the time and effort needed to make shifts as per conditions.

A Brief History of Scrum

Project management is hardly new.

As a matter of fact, traditional project management was born out of the experiences that project professionals had as a result of their work in various fields. Since project management was largely experienced-based, it wasn't always easy for project managers to deal with the myriad of aspects that go into completing a project successfully.

13

Over time, project management became more systematic in such a way that experiences were collected and built into a framework that could be used as a reference for future work done in similar fields.

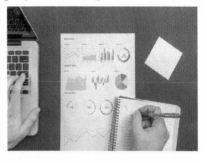

This collection of knowledge, experience, and lessons learned led to the creation of the traditional project management approaches known today. In particular, the methodology espoused by the Project Management Institute.

While there is nothing wrong with this methodology, the software industry realized that traditional project management approaches just weren't cutting it for them. There had to be something more suited to the needs and characteristics of the software industry which could provide a more dynamic framework.

And so, the nineties brought about innovations in the field of programming and software development. One of the new methods that emerged is known as "extreme programming" or XP. This led to one of the most popular versions of the Windows operating system known as "Windows XP."

Extreme programming became one of the precursors to what would eventually become known as Agile. Considering that Agile was born out of the software industry, Agile project management methodologies became synonymous with the software industry.

In the late nineties, some of the most successful software developers and programmers began putting their heads together in order to come up with a brand-new approach which could encompass the needs and characteristics of the software industry.

This led to the emergence of the Agile Manifesto in 2001.

The Agile Manifesto

The group of 17 minds which came together to develop the Agile Manifesto was intent on building a list of ideas and concepts in a framework which could serve their own industry. Nevertheless, the Agile Manifesto wasn't just about the software industry; it was intended to have a cross-cutting appeal which could lead it to be applied to virtually any known industry.

The Agile Manifesto is a collection of 12 principles which encompass the Agile philosophy. They make up the core and the backbone of all Agile methodologies in such a way that they are the guiding tenets on which Agile methodologies are founded on.

Since 2001, the Agile movement has grown into a series of methodologies which can be applied to a given number of roles. In that regard, Scrum is the one which has the most cross-cutting appeal. This is the kind of methodology which can be implemented in virtually any field, particularly, those that have a high degree of uncertainty and even volatility.

Therefore, Agile should be seen as a mindset more than a collection of steps which make up a procedure.

That's the case of traditional project management.

If you are looking for a collection of steps that must be implemented in succession without much consideration on how to innovate or implement change, then you should take a long look at how Scrum can also be used in a systematic and formulaic way.

Consequently, Agile has a little bit of everything for everyone. You won't have to guess at anything. However, Agile does require you to often think outside the box and not within a rigid structure. By freeing your mind, you will be able to see the forest for the trees and really find the best and most creative way of doing things.

This led the Agile Manifesto to become a declaration in which its creators stated the following:

"We are uncovering better ways of developing software by doing it and helping others do it. Through this work, we have come to value:

Individuals and interactions *over processes and tools*

Working software *over comprehensive documentation*

Customer collaboration *over contract negotiation*

Responding to change *over following a plan*

That is, while there is value in the items on the right, we value the items on the left more."

17

As you can see, the Agile Manifesto is a declaration in which its authors wanted to make clear what they value and where they stand on the development of outputs.

Of course, it should be noted that the Agile Manifesto explicitly talks about software and its development though we have clearly stated that from its software beginnings Agile is now applicable to virtually all fields.

Notice how Agile values people more than processes and tools. While processes and tools are important, Agile believes that people hold a greater value. The same can be said about working software, that is, a working output, over documentation that covers the project itself. Sure, there is paperwork to be dealt with, but rather than spending large amounts of time preparing complex reports and manuals that will probably have to been changed again in no time, focus on getting something valuable as a deliverable out to your customers.

The last two points in the Agile Manifesto refer to change and customer collaboration. This is important since engagement with the customer is essential in making sure that the outputs developed, meet the customer's expectations. Responding to change not only refers to what the customer wants but also what the circumstance may dictate. Therefore, Agile is all about flexibility and adaptability rather than setting everything in stone and "perfecting" the way things are done.

Now that Agile is a considered to be a full-fledged project management framework, it's worth looking at the principles which guide its implementation and development.

Principle #1: Our highest priority is to satisfy the customer through early and continuous delivery of valuable ~~software~~. *information*

This principle speaks for itself. The main idea behind this first principle is to meet the customer's expectation, but also to deliver working software early on in the development of the final product. This is an important difference over traditional project management methodologies as traditional approaches usually leave delivery of outputs until the end of the project. This often leads to issues along the way that could have been resolved early on but end up being addressed at the end.

This principle is applicable to all fields. It is quite possible to deliver results in advance of the release of the final output. By doing this, it enables the customer and project stakeholders to see where problems may lie, and how to address them before the final output is released.

As such, the starting point is to ensure customer satisfaction above all.

Principle #2: Welcome changing requirements, even late in development. Agile processes harness change for the customer's competitive advantage.

In traditional project management methodologies, change is discouraged as traditional project management tries to establish predictable processes as much as possible. The reason for this is rooted in the desire to eliminate uncertainty which can increase risk.

In the realm of Agile, change is welcome even if it is very late in the game. Of course, ground rules need to be set in order to govern change management. Nevertheless, Agile opens the door for changes to be made. After all, it's all about delivering the type of product which will give the customer an edge over their competition.

Consequently, Agile teams need to keep an open mind that leads them to figure out how to incorporate change without becoming clogged up with the reason why a change shouldn't be made. That is why providing deliverables at different stages are vital for successful project management.

Principle #3: Deliver working software [information] frequently, from a couple of weeks to a couple of months, with a preference to the shorter timescale.

Once again, Agile is bent on providing outputs as early as possible. When this happens, the customer can see what is being done. Therefore, this improves the quality of the communication and feedback that development teams can get on their work.

Thus, Agile teams should be encouraged to produce deliverables as early as possible in order to ensure that potential issues can be addressed well ahead of time and dealt with accordingly.

Principle #4: Business people and developers must work together daily throughout the project.

This principle underscores the highly collaborative nature of Agile. Rather than leaving the customer out of the development process, Agile encourages the customer's input and feedback as much as possible throughout the development cycle of the project.

In addition, the roles of the leaders in an Agile environment is to maintain constant communication with development teams in order to ensure that they have all of the resources they need while addressing any limitations that may have arisen from the normal course of action.

Principle #5: Build projects around motivated individuals. Give them the environment and support they need and trust them to get the job done.

Earlier, when I made a point of Agile being a mindset, I had this principle in mind.

21

When you think about "motivated individuals" it isn't just about people who want to work and get things done. That's not enough.

In Agile, the mindset needs to be focused on getting the job done in the best possible way, especially if that entails coming up with a novel solution. After all, creativity is at the heart of innovation. But this only happens when individuals are truly engaged with the role; they play on the team they are on.

So, motivation is built on empowering individuals to take control of their own area of responsibility. Bear in mind that Agile places greater value on individuals rather than processes. So, fostering individuals is at the core of developing an Agile mindset.

Principle #6: The most efficient and effective method of conveying information to and within a development team is a face-to-face conversation.

It should be noted that technology has made communication so much easier especially when teams are not physically located together. Nevertheless, the best means of communication is still a face-to-face conversation.

This is a vital point since the co-location of teams allows for an improved collaborative environment. So, I hope that you are beginning to see a trend in the underlying philosophy that makes up an Agile team and environment.

Effective information sharing

Principle #7: Working ~~software~~ is the primary measure of progress.

This one is a biggie. After all, the only way you can truly measure the success of a project is through the achievement of the projects deliverable(s). If you are unable to deliver what you set out to deliver, then the project is essentially a failure.

Naturally, the Agile principles themselves make an explicit mention of working software though this can be applied to any type of field in which there is an output that is to be produced. When your team is able to produce such deliverables, then you can gauge if your projects have actually met the expectations it was set out to meet.

One important thing to note is, if for some reason, project deliverables are not met, and then any issues can be addressed in the subsequent phase of the project. Therefore, the development team will have the opportunity to deal with it in time. While that may entail some additional work, it will go a long way toward solving the overall issue.

Principle #8: Agile processes promote sustainable development. The sponsors, developers, and users should be able to maintain a constant pace indefinitely.

23

The point of "sustainable development" is all about being realistic. When project teams develop a given tempo, they are expected to maintain it over long periods of time, or indefinitely. This is an essential quality of Agile.

When teams develop a realistic tempo which they can maintain over long periods of time, they will be able to achieve a high level of performance. But it should also be noted that teams are discouraged from working "too fast" or "too hard" as this would lead to an unsustainable pace. Ultimately, an unsustainable pace would lead teams to burnout and potentially create more problems than solutions.

Principle #9: Continuous attention to technical excellence and good design enhances agility.

When teams are able to continuously perfect their systems, procedures and technical expertise, projects will become easier and easier while being completed in a shorter period of time. This is why Agile fosters an environment in which development teams should be collaborative and kept together as much as possible.

As long as development teams can remain together and develop their capabilities in tandem, they will be able to make faster progress. Ultimately, development teams will have their processes down to such a point where it becomes second-nature.

However, the adaptable nature of Agile does not afford development teams too much time to get comfortable.

Principle #10: Simplicity - the art of maximizing the amount of work not done - is essential.

By learning that work not done is just as important as the work that is actually done, teams can become highly efficient. They are able to get a clear sense of what can be done and the best way in which they can minimize the amount of work that goes into achieving a given task.

That being said, it's important for project leaders to understand the need to cut out unnecessary work. A simple example of this is documentation. Agile espouses an approach in which voluminous documentation is discouraged in favor of the simple reporting which can provide project stakeholders with the right idea about where the project is headed.

Principle #11: The best architectures, requirements, and designs emerge from self-organizing teams.

On the subject of self-organizing teams, Agile is all about letting development teams work things out amongst themselves. In contrast to traditional project management in which leaders dictate the work to be done, Agile is focused on letting teams figure out what they need to do and the best way to do it. This allows for creativity to breed the best possible solutions to the problems at hand.

Principle #12: At regular intervals, the team reflects on how to become more effective, then tunes and adjusts its behavior accordingly.

The last principle of the Agile philosophy considers the need to reflect and improve upon mistakes. As with anything in life, nothing is perfect. That is why development teams working under the Agile flag need to consider the importance of sitting down and going over the good and bad in each development phase. This fosters an environment of accountability among all stakeholders in such a way that there is no need to have one leader bearing down on everyone else.

The feedback loop that is created within an Agile environment allows for teams to become closer and develop the type of collaboration which is essential in getting the job done in the best possible manner.

Well, that was quite a bit of information we dealt with in this chapter. I would encourage you to go over the principles presented herein as Agile begins with a fundamental shift in your and your organization's mindset. Even if you don't deal with projects in the traditional sense of the word, you can still implement an Agile mindset in such a way that your organization will become more open to change.

The most important thing to keep in mind is that your team is the most valuable resource you have at your disposal. Therefore, giving teams the freedom to self-organize is one of the most important success factors when working within an Agile approach.

Chapter 2: Breaking Down A Scrum Project

In this chapter, we will be looking at how a Scrum project actually works and the way that Scrum can be put to the test. So, we are going to be taking a look at how a Scrum project begins, where it is born, and an overview of the different parts and stages of the project.

In addition, we will be looking at the main components of a Scrum project. That way, you can become aware of the different inputs that a successful Scrum project needs in order to achieve its goals.

So, then let's get started.

What is a Project?

In short, a project is a temporary action that will produce a permanent outcome.

Based on that logic, a project is a response to a problem, or need, which has motivated those affected to seek a permanent solution through a temporary action.

Let's consider a classic situation.

Two towns are divided by a river. In order for folks to go from one town to the next, they need to drive for about an hour in order to go around the river. However, the closest route between both towns, which is crossing the river, would take 10 minutes.

So, both towns have agreed to build a bridge to connect both towns so that folks from both towns can easily reach both sides. In addition, each town has agreed to pay for half of the cost of building the bridge.

A commission was created with members from both towns to come up with a project to get the bridge completed. After meetings, the commission has decided what they want, where they want it and a rough estimate of how long it would take to get it done.

The commission also met with contractors who pitched their ideas and plans. After careful consideration, one contractor was selected. This contractor got to work and built the bridge in three months. The contract was paid for their construction work but agreed to sign a contract for the maintenance of the bridge.

In the end, the project was a success; flow between both towns increased, investment picked up, and everyone came out a winner.

In this example, we see a problem, which is a river dividing both towns thereby forcing them to drive a long way around to reach the other side. As a result, business wasn't as good as it could be, and folks were discouraged from visiting the other town.

The solution was to build a bridge. The temporary action was the construction of the building itself. After all, construction was completed in three months. We don't expect the construction of the building to be ongoing forever. We expect the construction to be over in a given period of time and the final product to be delivered.

As such, the temporary action (the construction of the bridge), provided a permanent solution to the problem (the bridge itself). This is a clear example of how a project is nothing more than a temporary action.

Yet, there is a great deal of work that goes into building the bridge itself. There is labor, and there are resources, (time, money, materials) which are needed in order to make the project a reality. Therefore, it's up to the project managers to do their best in order to make the project bear the fruit that it was intended to.

In this example, we chose a rather predictable output, as a bridge construction is hardly a new endeavor. Of course, engineers and planners have taken it upon themselves to make new designs and attempt different approaches. Some have worked while others have not. Nevertheless, the important thing is that out of a seemingly perfected process there is still the initiative for growth and change.

In those fields in which there is much less certainty (software development, pharma, biotech, social programs) there is far less predictability. Consequently, project managers need to find the best way in which they can deliver results as early as possible and make sure that these results are sustainable throughout the life of the project. This is where Agile really shines.

Project Phases

Projects are typically conceived as a process that must be followed in order to achieve a final output successfully. This is an important consideration as project managers tend to make an effort to systematize processes in order to remove as much risk and uncertainty as possible.

While it is true that risk is an inherent part of any project, working with clear guidelines and within a proper framework can reduce a great deal of risk. However, projects tend to have dynamic natures in which anything can happen.

As such, projects generally have five phases. Let's get into detail regarding each one.

1. **Planning**. The first phase of any project is the planning phase. In this phase, project managers will sit down the project sponsors and stakeholders in order to determine what the objectives are intended for the project. This is the part where interested parties will sit down, hammer out contracts, and come to agreements on what is going to be delivered, under what timeline and what the acceptance criteria for the project will be. This phase also considers the formation of project teams.

2. **Initiation**. The second phase of a project involves the necessary prep work that will go into putting the project into motion. This could include the purchase of equipment, hiring of staff, and the acquisition of any other materials which will be needed in order to make the project happen. Also, negotiations may be conducted with suppliers as needed.

3. **Execution**. This phase is all about getting the job done. So, the project teams will come together to actually work and get the project moving. Depending on the project management methodology, you might get some early results such as in the of Agile, or deliverables will be seen until

the end of the project such as in the case of more traditional project management approaches. This is the phrase in which the objectives begin to come to fruition.

4. **Monitoring and evaluation.** When the project reaches this phase, it is because the final output has been released and is undergoing testing. It is at the point that the final deliverables are tested to make sure they meet the required specifications before the final acceptance of the products. This phase may lead to the customer rejecting the final product and requesting changes before the final product is accepted.

5. **Closing.** Once the products have been accepted, then the project will go into the closing phase. When the project enters this phase, any final changes are made to the deliverables, and the customer gives the final acceptance to the products. This is where the ribbon is cut, and all the applauses come. The final release of the product is issued, and there are high fives all around. The project team then begins to wind everything up and either move on to the next project or say goodbye.

This process described above is the typical lifecycle of the project. This type of process can normally be seen with traditional project management methodologies. In such cases, you will notice that testing and acceptance happens at the end of the entire project cycle. This means that the customer will not have any indication of what the final product will look like until the end of the project itself.

This approach opens the door for a series of issues since the project team will not be clear on what will happen when the customer sees the final output. As such, there is a very real possibility that the customer will not accept the final deliverables and ask for changes. When this happens, it can become catastrophic to the project team as having changes made to the deliverables once they have been assembled may lead to considerable cost and time overruns. Consequently, making sure that the final outputs are produced to the specifications of the client is essential in order to avoid any delays or even surprises at the end of the project.

How Does Scrum Play into All of This?

Scrum works in the exact same way as normal project work. The main difference between a traditional project and Scrum is in the mindset and attitude toward change, adaptability, and harnessing the power of change.

Naturally, Scrum begins with a planning phase that leads to the initiation phase. Once the project is off and running, the development team can come in and get to work. However, the main difference with Scrum is that the execution phrase is broken down into sections called "sprints." These sprints are designed to be phases in which the development team produce a certain aspect of the final output. At the end of the sprint, the customer should be able to see that part in action, in order to get a glimpse of what the final product will look like.

The monitoring and evaluation phase are integrated into each sprint in such a way that the development team can test the product and determine if there are mods which need to be made to ensure that everything is running fine. Finally, the closing phrase will lead to the customer accepting the final output and thereby bringing the project to an end.

Since every project is different, the project team needs to be prepared for anything that may come their way. This means keeping an open mind and ensuring that they have everything they need in order to become as successful as they possibly can. Nevertheless, care needs to be taken in ensuring that the most important aspects of the final output are respected.

As you can see, the biggest difference in terms of the organization that a Scrum project has compared to a traditional one, is that Scrum is focused on the customer, delivering value as early as possible and working out any potential bugs from the get-go. This ensures that all stakeholders will be aware of how the project is developing.

By addressing potential issues as early as possible, the project team can see if there might be any time or cost overruns and see how they may be addressed. Furthermore, the project team can determine what needs to be in order to avoid cost and time overruns. That way, the project can become successful, meet the acceptance criteria, and deliver on the overall objectives as stated.

Scrum Project Components

At this point, we are going to get into the specifics of the components which make up a Scrum project.

First of all, let's look at the players that make up a Scrum team.

- **Product Owner**. The Product Owner in a Scrum team is called "the voice of the customer." What this means is that the developers won't actually have any direct communication with the customer. That's the Product Owner's job. The Product Owner is the main person in charge of interacting with the customer in such a way that the Product Owner is able to relay the customer's vision and feedback to the rest of the team. This implies that the Product Owner is at the front line of the development process. And while the Product Owner has a key leadership role, they are not the boss.

- **Scrum Master**. The name of this player does not refer to "master" in terms of domain or leadership, but rather, it refers to the level of mastery in the Scrum methodology. As such, the

Scrum Master is the link between the Product Owner (the customer) and the Development Team. The role of the Scrum Master is that of subservient leadership. That is, the Scrum Master is very much engaged in providing guidance and leadership when needed but does not act like a "boss." Rather, the Scrum Master's role is to provide all of the necessary tools and elements which the Development Team needs in order to carry out their objectives.

• **Development Team**: The Development Team is the one in charge of actually putting the project into motion. These are the folks who actually carry out the work. In general, a Development Team consists of about 4 to 6 members. They generally work in a co-located setting, that is, in the same physical location under the guidance of the Scrum Master and Product Owner. The Development Team is also in charge of conducting product demos and technical explanations to the customer especially when the Product Owner is not the most qualified to deliver such information.

As you can see, the number of players in a Scrum team is rather small. As such, one of the biggest criticisms of Scrum is that it is not scalable particularly for very large and extensive projects. But that assertion could not be further from the truth.

When dealing with very large-scale projects, Scrum can be scaled in such a way that multiple Development Team teams work in tandem with multiple Scrum Masters in order to break up the work into a manageable chunk.

In fact, very large projects may have broader roles such as a Project Product Owner and a Project Scrum Master. These two roles would be in charge of making sure the entire project machinery works in tandem.

While we will get into further details about Scrum roles in later chapters, it's worth pointing out that the description we have provided herein helps to gain a better perspective of how Agile, and in particular Scrum, see the interaction between the various players throughout the lifecycle of the project.

It should also be noted that Scrum strives to achieve efficiency by having the greatest amount of work done with the least amount of staff.

Now, does this mean that staff will be pushed to the max?

Actually, no.

Bear in mind that Scrum advocates for a sustainable tempo. What that means is that the Development Team needs to be pushed to reasonable limits. Thus, you cannot expect the Development Team to be working 12 hours a day and maintain that kind of pace over extended amounts of time. Of course, there are times when such things may be needed.

Supposing that for some reason the project should fall behind schedule, the Development Team must work at the best pace possible while the Scrum Master and the Product Owner figure out the best way in which to improve tempo and make up for lost time.

Also, keep in mind that Agile does not allow for falling behind schedule. If anything, Agile seeks to deliver ahead of schedule. Though delivering ahead of schedule is not a priority, it is preferred over falling behind.

This is why both the Scrum Master and the Product Owner must consider that pushing the Development Team to the max might not be the best course of action as this could lead the team to burnout and create a lot more complications for the project than anticipated.

There is one other character that is not normally included in a regular Scrum team but can come into the picture if needed. This character is called an "Agile Coach." An Agile Coach, as the name states, is a coach who can guide Scrum team members in the proper application of Scrum principles and methodology. This coach can come in handy especially when teams are brand new to Scrum and haven't fully developed the practice they need. So, the Agile Coach can "correct" mistakes and make sure that the Development Team adheres to the specifications of a Scrum project.

The Agile Coach is an expert who has experience in all three tiers of the Scrum project management domain. Ideally, the Agile coach would have experience as a developer thus providing them with the necessary knowledge and understanding of what a typical Development Team goes through. The Agile Coach may come and go as needed or work full-time with the Development Team while they learn the ropes of the Scrum methodology.

What is a "Sprint"?

Earlier, we discussed the various phases of a project. These phases are the natural process by which the work breakdown takes place within a project. Consequently, each phase contemplates different activities which are generally interdependent. Therefore, you cannot move on from one phase to another without completing the requisite groundwork. What this implies is that Scrum teams need to have a clear understanding of how the tasks from one sprint are needed in order to build on to the next one.

Sprints take place during the execution phase of the project in which the work that is done is actually conducive to producing the final product. As such, the Development Team takes center stage during each sprint. The Scrum Master and Product Owner play a secondary, supporting role in which they are there to make sure that the Development Team has everything they need in order to get the job done.

During sprints, it is highly uncommon to see the Product Owner involved in the actual work being delivered unless it is absolutely necessary due to extemporaneous reasons. The leader who is in charge of making sure everything goes according to schedule is the Scrum Master.

Thus, the Scrum Master is the player that looks at where potential issues may arise and find proactive ways of addressing them if they can be addressed ahead of schedule. If issues happen to be unforeseen for whatever reason, then the Scrum Master must deal with them, usually in coordination with the Product Owner, in order to allow the Development Team to keep working.

The only case in which the Development Team should stop working is in the case of a catastrophic event that would render the entire project inoperable. Nevertheless, reaching a point such as this would be an extreme case that no one in their right mind would have been able to predict.

Notwithstanding, sprints generally last between 2 to 6 weeks with the average sprint length being 4 weeks or a month, give or take a day or two.

The reason for this particular sprint length is that 4 weeks seems to be the ideal time for Development Teams to actually produce results. If sprints are shorter, then it would be harder to produce accurate results while having longer sprints may lead to time being wasted.

Of course, given Scrum's adaptable nature, if a 4-week sprint is too short given the dynamic of the project, then the Scrum Master and Product Owner may choose to go for a longer sprint the next time around. If they feel that there was time left over, then more work could be incorporated into the next sprint as opposed to shortening the following one.

It should also be noted that sprints may vary in length throughout the entire project. So, you could have a shorter, 3-week sprint at the outset of the project and then have 5-week sprints at other points in the project. While this is possible, it is not recommended as it could upset the Development Team's tempo and rhythm. So, the ideal way to go would be to keep sprint lengths as even as possible.

Sprints are built on iteration. This means that sprints have a repetitive nature in which each sprint will have the same steps and procedures done. What this does is provide a certain level of predictability into how each sprint is conducted. Considering that Scrum plays in a highly unstable and uncertain environment, incorporating some measure of certainty is ideal for Development Teams to build around.

In the next chapter, we will get into even more detail on how each sprint works. The most important takeaway at this point lies in understanding that a sprint is the main scheduling tool that is used to plan the work to be carried out in a project.

The Project Charter

During a Scrum project, a Project Charter is created during the planning phase.

The negotiating and drafting of the Project Charter are the responsibility of the Product Owner. It is written well before any of the multiple components of the project are put into place. In fact, the Project Charter may be written before the Scrum Master and Development Team is put into place.

So, what is a "Project Charter"?

In traditional project management, a Project Charter would be the contract that the customer signs with the company that is going to carry out the project. As such, Scrum does not advocate for a contract in itself, but rather, a document that reads more like a Memorandum of Understanding in which all of the ground rules are laid out for the governance of the project.

Therefore, the Project Charter will contain everything pertaining to the duration of the project, the deliverables, acceptance criteria, payment details, and any other provisions which the stakeholders deem necessary and appropriate.

The Project Charter, in itself, is not a legally binding document. Rather, it is a document of good faith that enables all participants to have clear rules about how the project will be governed. This plays into one of the principles of Agile which espouses working software over complex documentation.

Now, there will more than likely be a need for formal, legally binding contracts. In that case, the Product Owner will seek the necessary legal counsel that will take care of drafting the contracts based on the Project Charter. While it is the responsibility of the Product Owner to draft the Project Charter, it is not the Product Owner's responsibility of drafting contracts unless they are licensed attorneys.

The Project Charter must then be approved by the customer or stakeholder(s) commissioning the project. Upon approval, the Project Charter comes into force and becomes the official document that will govern the entire project's development.

Since there is no official template that is used to draft a Project Charter, I recommend drafting it a like Memorandum of Understanding in which it is explicitly stated that all of the stakeholders in the project agree on the clauses contained in the document and commit to upholding them at all times. There must also be clauses added pertaining to conflict resolution. While you would not be expecting the conflict to occur, you do want to make sure that it is included so that all sides are covered in case there is ever any kind of dispute among the parties.

Finally, the Project Charter, as the law of the land, must be discussed among all members of the Project Team so that they are clear about what they are expected to do and how they must do it. The Product Owner may also craft mini charters outlining the role of each member of the Development Team. This can be a useful tool especially when there are cases of Development Team members unclear whether an activity exceeds their scope of responsibility or not.

User Stories

Another of the Product Owner's main responsibilities the development of the so-called "user stories."

A user story is a detailed description of the needs for each part of the project, to help the team come up with the most appropriate solution. As such, user stories are like putting a name and a face to who will actually benefit from the project.

Let's consider an example.

The main output of the project will be a mobile fitness app. The app will track health-related stats such as the number of steps, time at the gym, eating habits and so on. The project has kicked off with a Project Charter signed and approved.

The Product Owner is now in an information gathering phase in which the customer has expressed what they need but are not exactly sure what the final product will be like. In addition, they are not entirely sure of who their core consumers will be.

Therefore, it's up to the Product Owner to come up with a user story based on what the customer has specified. As such, the customer's specifications call for the app to be directed at young adults who work in a high-pace environment and don't have a lot of time and attention for fitness. So, the app is intended to provide reminders pertaining to drinking enough water, taking a break to stretch and so on.

With this in mind, the Product Owner can come up with a user story detailing who that specific user will be. Consequently, a user story can look something like this:

"Joe is a 28-year-old bank employee who typically works 12-hour days. He is single and lives with his dog in a one-bedroom apartment located in the downtown area of a large metropolitan city. He walks to work every day as his office is about 15 minutes away. He prefers to walk rather than take public transportation since the walk allows him to get exercise. He is health conscious but doesn't always have time to follow a strict diet. He is also very technologically inclined. He tries to use his smartphone for virtually everything he can."

This user story is just a sample. It could be even more detailed. In fact, the higher the level of detail, the better the context it will provide the Development Team in creating the app with these characteristics in mind. User stories can also be very specific to describe a feature, such as:

"*As a* user, *I want to* see how many steps I've taken each day and how that compares to previous days, *so that* I can track my physical activity, *in order to* lose weight."

Once the Product Owner has come up with this user story, the customer will have a look at it and request changes or sign off on it. Once the customer is happy with it, the Product Owner is now ready to get the ball rolling on the development of the app itself.

Now, there are a couple of twists here: The Product Owner could choose to do the entire user story process alone or choose to hire the Scrum Master in order to craft it together. Another option is where the Product Owner hires the entire Scrum team and develops the user stories as a collaborative team process. This is actually a good idea especially when the Product Owner does not have a great deal of expertise with the product being developed.

It should be noted that the Product Owner does not need to be an expert in the actual product being developed but does need to be an experienced Scrum practitioner. The Scrum Master should at least have a working knowledge of what the product is and what its development process is like. The ones who should be experts in the product being developed are the members of the Development Team.

One final note on user stories: user stories are based on real customers who will use the product once it's released. As such, the Product Owner may choose to talk to potential customers in order to get a feel for what they want. There could be focus group discussions, interviews and any other kind of research needed in order to gain the intelligence needed to create a viable user story.

Acceptance Criteria

Finally, the last component in a Scrum project is the acceptance criteria that the customer has outlined in order to determine the product's level of quality. If the acceptance criteria are not met, then the Scrum team must go back and figure out what's wrong. Though it should be noted that acceptance criteria are taken into account throughout the entire development process. Therefore, if the Development Team keeps these parameters in mind, there shouldn't be complications in actually achieving the acceptance criteria.

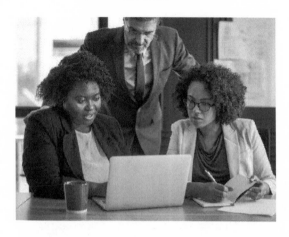

Acceptance criteria can come in the way of specific functionalities that the product provides. This can be written either as a checklist or as an extension of a user story. In the previous example, we talked about a fitness app. So, an example of acceptance criteria for this fitness app could be:

"*Given* I have walked 10,000 steps, *When* I hit this target, I get a notification through the app."

Other acceptance criteria could be automatic reminders for medication and vitamins. It may also include spoken alerts saying, "it's time to drink water." Of course, that is something that the customer would specify, and the Development Team must produce.

Now, it should also be noted that the Development Team should not produce anything that is not asked for. This means resisting the temptation to "improve" upon the customer's ideas.

Why?

Unsolicited features and functionalities may lead to useless work. The customer may not appreciate the added features or may even question why it was added in the first place. This can lead to wasted time and resources. Any "improvements" should be brought up the Development Team through the Scrum Master so that the Product Owner can speak to the customer and let them know what the Development Team wants to do and why they want to do it.

Once the customer is aware of what is going to be done and why it is needed, the Development Team can proceed with confidence. This is the type of ongoing communication that all sides need to maintain. Of course, since no one is perfect, there may be situations that were overlooked at the outset of the project, but which became apparent during the product's development. So, the Development Team can bring up their issues and concerns and let them be known.

Acceptance criteria are laid out in the Project Charter and can be listed as a checklist for the Development Team's benefit. With the user stories, acceptance criteria and the functionalities requested by the customer, the Development Team can work together to decide how they will achieve the acceptance criteria and produce the results.

Since Scrum teams are self-governing, the Development Team itself can decide how they want to approach the development of the product. The Scrum Master will only serve as a moderator throughout the process and take note of what is needed in order to get the job done.

The final details of the work to be done will be highlighted in the Scrum Burndown chart. The Scrum Master and especially the Product Owner, work on the sidelines ensuring that everything is going according to schedule.

In subsequent chapters, we will be going into very specific detail about what happens during a sprint and how each of the players interacts with one another. In addition, we will provide some practical examples that should help you to better understand the way Scrum projects are conducted in a typical, day-to-day environment.

Product Owner speaks Dave for members

Scrum master moderates pla. Karen

Dev. Team - Execute Tasks Holly + Mel

Chapter 3: Sprints Within A Scrum Project

In this chapter, we will go deep into what a Scrum sprint is, how it works, and what elements make up a typical sprint. Also, we will be providing examples in addition to contrasting how a typical sprint stacks up against traditional project management processes.

Sprints within a Scrum project are essentially individual parts of the execution phase of a project. As stated earlier, the execution phase of the project is where the actual work is done. As such, it is where the products are developed, and the project's objectives are completed.

The initial sprint in a Scrum project begins when the Project Charter is approved by the customer, and the user stories are ready. Of course, the project team also needs to be in place in order for work to get started.

It should be noted that it's up to the Product Owner to determine how soon the project team will be put together. And there is no specific order in which the team should be put together. A traditional approach would be to have the Product Owner choose the Scrum Master and then the Product Owner and Scrum Master choose the Development Team in tandem.

However, this is not always the case. It could be that the Product Owner chooses the Development Team and then chooses a Scrum Master based on the Development Team. So, the Product Owner can choose the players on their team based on what the project is about and how it could be developed.

Let's look at a couple of examples of how a Scrum team can be put together.

First, let's assume that the project idea is born within a company, but the project team will be completely external from the company. Therefore, the company that is looking to put this project to work will be looking for an external consulting firm that can help them implement the project.

Now, this company is looking to implement a project for the improvement of a completely new employee benefits scheme. In this case, this is something the company has never done before. While it did have a traditional employee benefits scheme based on performance bonuses and holiday time, it is clear to the company directors that something a little more modern needs to be put into place.

So, the CEO of the company has received the Board's permission to go ahead and implement a new employee benefits scheme that revolves around a series of fringe benefits and other non-monetary incentives that can boost employee morale and thereby boost productivity.

Since the company is unsure about how to implement this project, the Human Resources department has indicated that since they are understaffed and behind on most of their work, they would rather only take a lesser consulting role.

As such, the company's directors have agreed to the hiring of an outside consultant who could oversee the implementation of the new employee benefits scheme. Since the time is at a premium, the Board is anxious to get the full system implemented in about 8 weeks. The reason for this time slot is because there are roughly two months left before the end of the current quarter. So, the directors feel that it would be great to get the new scheme in place right before the start of the new quarter.

The Human Resources manager has been tasked with finding the right person for the job. Through some recommendations, a great consultant was found. This consultant has ample experience in the restructuring of companies. So, this individual seemed like a good fit. And, this consultant is also a Scrum practitioner.

This consultant has met with the directors of the company, and they have all agreed that it would be best to bring in unbiased individuals from the outside. This would make it easier for the project team to make objective decisions since they don't have a personal stake in the company.

The first thing that the consultant has done is to take on the Product Owner role. This individual has decided that Scrum is the best way to go since there is no clear indication of how the new benefits scheme would work, and what the reactions of the company's current employees would be.

Therefore, the Product Owner has decided to get started by drafting up the Project Charter. This chapter contains all of the stipulations that will govern the life of the project. In addition, the consultant has had a lawyer draft up a legal contract in which all of the provisions contained in the Project Charter are officially signed and agreed upon.

Once the charter is signed, the company has agreed to give the consultant one week to get the project team together and kick off the project. Given this consultant's experience with projects in the past, the consultant has placed a few calls to some friends who might be interested in the Scrum Master's role. After a couple of calls, a qualified candidate has agreed to join the project.

The new Scrum Master has technical expertise in financial matters. In addition, these two individuals have worked together in the past. So, it makes sense that they join forces once more in this new endeavor.

The next step is to get the Development Team together. After some conversation and discussion, both the Product Owner and the Scrum Master have agreed that they need four members for the Development Team. They have decided what role each individual will play and what sort of expertise they need.

In this case, they have decided that they need four experienced individuals in the areas of Finance and Human Resources. Ideally, each candidate would have expertise in both areas, but they will settle if they have experience in just the one area. In any event, having two members with experience in Finance and two with experience in Human Resources would be acceptable too.

In addition, the payment terms in the Project Charter afford the hiring of four members of the Development Team, in addition to the compensation for the Product Owner and the Scrum Master. So, money also plays a role in determining the size of the team.

At this point, the Product Owner, Scrum Master, and the Development Team have all been assembled and are ready to get started working collaboratively. Their first order of business is to develop the user stories that will become part of the finished product that will be delivered to the customer.

The reason behind the Product Owner's decision to have the entire team work on the user stories is because the Development Team has ample experience in determining what would be good inputs for the new benefits scheme.

In order to get the user stories done quickly, the Product Owner has also decided to have one mega-meeting in which the entire project team would hammer out any, and all, user stories in one 8-hour session.

At the end of this session, and a couple of pizzas, three user stories came about.

The first user story is intended for the employees who have recently joined the company, that is, who have less than 1 year in the company. These employees make about roughly 20% of the company's workforce. So, they do represent a decent chunk of the payroll.

The second user story is intended for employees who have been with the company for over a year, but less than five years. These employees have enjoyed the company's previous benefit scheme but have also complained the most about it. As such, these are the employees who will be hit the hardest with the new changes that will occur. This group makes up over 50% of the workforce in the company.

The third user story is intended for those employees who have been with the company for over 5 years. This group makes up the remaining 30% of the workforce and represent a considerable amount of leadership positions within the company. They have also enjoyed the company's previous benefit scheme though it is unclear how they will react to the proposed changes.

Each user story has been drafted in such a way that every one of the groups highlighted has a name and a face that characterizes them. These were crafted out of the information the project team got from the company itself in addition to the project team's previous experience. With this, the project team is now set to work on the project and ready to make progress.

This is the first example I would like to provide you with on how to make up a Scrum team. As you can see, the entire team is external and foreign to the inner workings of the company. Consequently, they should be free to think outside the box and come up with novel solutions for the needs of this company.

Now, let's consider the second way in which the company could put together its project team based on a Scrum mentality.

The CEO got the green light from the Board on the project. The CEO has asked the Human Resources Manager to be the project lead. This was more an imposition than anything else. However, the company has offered the Human Resources Manager, as well as any other member in the company who participates in the project, a bonus for their work on this project.

Since the Human Resources manager has been trained in Scrum, they understand how the process works and are keen on delivering the best possible outcome for the customer.

After being officially notified of what the company's expectations are for the project, the Human Resources manager has decided to take on the role of Product Owner. This manager will be the main interlocutor between the CEO and the Development Team.

The next step is to find the Scrum Master.

The Product Owner has identified a colleague from the Finance department who is very knowledgeable about payroll and restructuring in addition to having an understanding of Scrum. After getting approval from the Finance Manager and the CEO, the Product Owner has a new Scrum Master.

Together, the Product Owner and the Scrum Master have come up with the Project Charter. The reason for doing this exercise like this is to cover all of the aspects which ought to govern the project. After a good morning's worth of work, the Project Charter is set. The CEO reads it, makes some observations, changes are made, and the Project Charter is officially in place.

Now it's time to put the Development Team together.

The Product Owner has convinced the CEO to let them pull four members from the various departments into the company as full-time developers. The CEO has reluctantly agreed to let them work on the project full-time for four weeks. So, that means that the Development Team has four weeks to put the entire plan together and produce the outputs the project intends to produce.

As such, this would only provide one month, or what could basically be just the one sprint.

So, the four employees chosen for the project were selected based on their experience, knowledge of Scrum and their dedication to the project. Since the CEO agreed to give an additional bonus to whoever took part in the project, the selected members of the Development Team seemed to be very motivated to get started.

With this, the Product Owner has its team in place.

However, since the Product Owner feels that the having the Development Team participate in creating the user stories is inappropriate due to their personal stake in the project (they will benefit from a new benefit scheme), the Product Owner has decided to create the user stories alone.

Once the user stories have been crafted and approved, the project is now officially set to get underway.

In this example, the Scrum team came from within the company. This means that the company won't have to pay an external consultant to do the job. Although, it does represent a cost to the company as they will be away from their usual jobs for the next four weeks.

Also, the Product Owner has the option of hiring an Agile Coach to guide them through the process of this new project. The Board has agreed to hire such a coach as this would enable the team to work out any questions they may have about Scrum or any other aspects which could be improved.

This example underscores a rather unconventional way in which a team can be put together. In total 6 employees were plucked away from their regular jobs. That is, the Product Owner, who is the Human Resources manager, still has their regular job to worry about. But since being a Product

Owner does not require full-time participation in the actual activities, it allows the Human Resources manager to carry on their work.

Of course, the Scrum Master and the development team are working full-time as they only have four weeks to get the job done. In addition, since Scrum calls for co-located teams, the Product Owner has given them a vacant office to use as a meeting room/war room where they can work together to get the job done. Thus, the project management is on the clock and must deliver the first results in the next couple of weeks.

The two, previous examples underscore the importance of having a solid Development Team that is eager to get started. They can come in and get started at any time while allowing the entire project team to feel comfortable about the work that is going to be done.

Getting That First Sprint off the Ground

In Scrum, there are a series of meetings which take place at various intervals. These meetings are what make the Scrum methodology work.

When the first sprint is set to get started, the project team will have what is called a "Sprint

Planning Meeting." In this meeting, the entire Scrum team will sit down and go over the work breakdown for the sprint, what to expect, and any concerns that are on the minds of the members. In addition, work is prioritized and estimated on the time needed for each of the activities. This is called "timeboxing," and it is a rigid standard by which all of the members of the team must adhere to.

At this point, the Sprint Planning Meeting is the only one which the Product Owner is required to attend until the end of the sprint. The Scrum Master should attend all meetings while the Development Team must be engaged in every single one of these meetings.

Once the work breakdown has been agreed upon, the sprint is set to begin. Ideally, it would begin on the first day of the work week, so there is a logical starting point to the sprint and conclude on the last workday of the workweek in which the project concludes.

Each of the members is now ready to get to work and begin carrying out the tasks they have agreed to. Bear in mind that Scrum teams are self-organizing. So, the team itself decides who does what, how long it should take, and how the end result of the tasks would be.

Every working day begins with the "Daily Standup Meeting." This meeting is done on a daily basis and is intended to provide every team member with the opportunity to voice any concerns, ask for help, request anything they might need and talk about what they expect to get done on that day.

This should last no more than 15 minutes. The Product Owner is not required to attend the Daily Standup Meeting, though the Scrum Master is most certainly required to attend. Each of the team members will have a chance to speak while the Scrum Master takes note of what is being discussed.

The Daily Standup Meeting also serves as a log of the items discussed and provides the Scrum Master with a registry of the thoughts expressed by the Development Team. This registry should provide insights into upcoming sprints and other projects.

In addition, the Scrum Master and Product Owner should have at least one weekly meeting in which all of these concerns are expressed. This will allow the Product Owner to brief the customer on the progress being while gaining perspective from the customer as to what the customer expects from the project.

Now, let's assume that the sprint lasted four weeks. So, at the end of the sprint, the "Sprint Review Meeting" is held. This meeting is essentially a demonstration that is provided to the stakeholders in the project so that they may see the advances that have been produced as part of the previous sprint. This is a good chance for the customer to provide any feedback, through the Product Owner, and which the Development Team can take into account while continuing to develop the final outputs of the project.

The Sprint Review Meeting is also the official ending of the sprint. With that, the Development Team is now ready to move on to the next sprint. While it is not recommended for there to be any kind of a break, the Product Owner and Scrum Master may agree to let them off for a long weekend just to let them disconnect from the project especially if the previous sprint had been demanding.

The next meeting that takes place is the "Sprint Retrospective Meeting."

In this meeting, the entire Scrum team is together. The Product Owner can provide the customer's feedback on the demonstrations conducted, while the Scrum Master can also go over any of the observations made during the sprint. Each of the Development Team members has the opportunity to express what they felt was done right and what they feel could be improved.

In addition, "mistakes" must be addressed at this meeting so that they can be "corrected" in the upcoming sprint. Also, the Product Owner and Scrum Master can go over any change requests the customer has made so that these changes may be incorporated in the next sprint.

As such, Scrum practitioners should note, especially Product Owners, that change requests from the customer should not be implemented mid-sprint. This may end up disrupting the tempo that the Development Team has achieved. This is why the Product Owner must be clear that with the sprint underway, it is very difficult to shift course and meet deadlines.

Consequently, any change requests should be implemented in the following sprint so that there is a logical break in the tempo of the work being conducted and the Development Team has a chance to plan how they will tackle that change.

The only reason change requests should be admitted mid-sprint is if there is some type of urgent need. This could be due to many factors. But the bottom line is that only a major event could trigger a change request mid-sprint.

Once the Sprint Retrospective Meeting is done, the Scrum team should move onto the next Sprint Planning Meeting. So, assuming that the Sprint Retrospective Meeting was conducted on a Friday afternoon, the next Sprint Planning Meeting can be conducted first thing Monday morning. Once the next Sprint Planning Meeting is in the books, then the next sprint may officially begin.

One question that often comes up: how many sprints should there be in a project?

The simple answer is that there need to be as many sprints as are required by the customer's request and the estimate on the time and work breakdown. Consequently, it's very difficult to say that each project should last two sprints or three sprints.

In the end, it all depends on the type of project you are working on and the type work to be done. This is why many Product Owners will have their team in place before committing to timelines. That way, they can be sure that the time estimate set is the best one based on the experience of the Development Team.

Scrum Artifacts

Do you recall the Agile principle that values working software over comprehensive documentation?

Well, Agile and Scrum do have some documentation which needs to be taken care of. The main difference is that the documentation generated in Scrum isn't as extensive as in other project management methodologies.

As such, there is a set of documentation which is generated that serves to keep a log of the actions that are done. The reason for keeping this log is to track and monitor the development of the tasks being done as they are completed throughout the course of a sprint. These logs then serve to provide stakeholders with information on the status of the project.

The Product Backlog

In short, the Product Backlog is everything that is going to be completed in a project.

Now, the Product Backlog should not be confused with the final output. The final output could be working software. So, the Product Backlog is all of the actions that need to be done in order to reach that final outcome.

The Product Backlog is the responsibility of the Product Owner. Although, it is recommended that the Product Backlog is built as part of a collaborative effort by the entire Scrum team. The reason for this is that the Development Team can estimate whether or not given tasks are really needed. The evaluation on the part of the Development Team can determine if the tasks to be conducted make sense or if other tasks need to be implemented as well.

When the Product Backlog is created as part of a collaborative effort, the entire Scrum team can feel empowered because they had a say in the activities and tasks that are to make up the project. Also, it is quite possible that Development Team members have experience which they can put to good use during the project itself.

The Product Backlog can simply be a grocery list of tasks which need to be completed. The main thing to keep in mind, though, is that even if it's just a list, the interdependencies among the various tasks need to be established. This will allow for the Development Team to understand which tasks need to be done first in order to build on them and move onto subsequent tasks.

It's also worth noting that the Product Backlog should lead the Scrum team to determine which actions will happen in which sprints. Thus, the need for identifying interdependencies is crucial in developing a proper work breakdown structure, not just for each sprint, but for the entire project itself.

In addition, the Project Backlog will end up becoming the checklist by which the Scrum team will determine the progress being made.

The Sprint Backlog

Once the Product Backlog has been established, then the Sprint Backlog can be created. This backlog is a list of the tasks which will be completed in that given sprint. The Sprint Backlog is created at the Sprint Planning Meeting.

When the Sprint Backlog is created, the tasks that will be completed are created, and then they are assigned to the various team members. This provides a clear discipline as to who will tackle what, leading the team to have a clear understanding of what needs to be accomplished during that sprint.

It should be noted that the tasks chosen in a given sprint should lead toward providing the customer with a glimpse of what the final product will be especially in its early stages. While demonstrating fully functioning software during the first sprint may not always be possible, it is certainly possible to consider producing an advance that will enable the customer to see where the product is going.

Product Backlog Item

A Product Backlog item is a specific task that needs to be completed as part of the overall achievement of the project outcomes. Usually, each Product Backlog item is comprised of several smaller tasks which build up to it.

Now, one large Product Backlog item could become the focus on an entire sprint in which the smaller tasks are completed by each team member. Also, a Product Backlog item might be the sole responsibility of one team member. As such, the team member will perform tasks in each sprint leading up to the final implementation of that Product Backlog item.

One interesting comparison between Product Backlog items with traditional project management methodologies is that Product Backlog items would be considered to project objectives. As such, project objectives tend to have an overarching presence throughout the entire execution of the project. Consequently, it's important to keep in mind that Product Backlog items are more general and provide guidance to the tasks at hand.

Sprint Tasks

Sprint tasks are the individual tasks that are to be achieved during a sprint. These tasks have an important function in the development of the project as their achievement will lead to the overall construction of the final deliverables.

Sprint tasks can be individually assigned to specific developers or can be developed in tandem. The main point to keep in mind is that sprint tasks need to be completed during that sprint. They cannot carry over into subsequent sprints. If the team is unable to complete a task, for whatever reason, then this needs to be addressed at the Sprint Retrospective Meeting. It would also be part of the Scrum Master's job description to find a proper solution for it.

During the Sprint Planning Meeting, the Scrum team will decide which tasks will be included in that sprint and then proceed to time box it. The team must be clear on how long each task will take, what work needs to be done in order to achieve it, and how many members need to work on each task. Ideally, you could have one member per task though that may not always be possible.

This is the reason why the decision of what to include in each sprint needs to be a collaborative decision, taking the input from developers as the most important criteria. Unless developers are completely new to Scrum, they will have an idea of how to handle the workflow they are going to take on.

Sprint Burndown Chart

The Sprint Burndown Chart is a visual representation of the progress being made in throughout the sprint. As tasks move from one part of the chart to the next, the team can get a sense of how the project is coming along.

As such, the chart measures the amount of work already done versus the time left. In a perfect world, the trend line generated by the chart should have a downward trend at a 45° angle. If this is the case, then the sprint is right on schedule. If it is trending sideways, then there is no progress being made, while a vertical trend line means that all of the tasks have been completed at the same time. Of course, such a thing is not possible.

Other times, the trend line in a Sprint Burndown chart may look like stairs. That this, one flat line moving sideways, followed by a vertical drop, and then another line moving sideways. This trend is perfectly fine and shows clear evidence of progress.

The Sprint Burndown chart should be seen as the definitive measure of the Development Team's progress. Therefore, it should be updated by the Scrum Master as tasks get done and results are being seen.

Product Burndown Chart

The Product Burndown Chart is the main tracker of the tasks being completed. This chart tracks the completion of the Backlog items. In short, it is a tracker for the completion of each sprint. Therefore, this chart serves as a measure for the team to see how far along they are in the overall completion of the project. It also allows the customer to see how far the project has come along.

This chart is generally updated by the Scrum Master, though it could be updated by the Product Owner as a part of the normal course of action at the end of each sprint. Although, it is highly recommended that it should be updated each time a Product Backlog item is completed.

As with the Sprint Burndown Chart, the trend line will determine how the project is coming along. Once this chart has been completed, then the project is essentially over and ready for the final acceptance criteria to be met.

Final Thoughts

Well, that was quite a bit of information we dealt with. I know that this may be a lot to take in, but I assure you that if you go step by step, you will be able to get a very good grasp of how a sprint starts and ends.

So, it is important for you to have a clear definition of all the tasks to be completed as part of the overarching Product Backlog items and how these can be broken down into the smaller, more specific Sprint tasks.

As each sprint is completed, the entire Scrum team, as well as the customer, will be able to see the actual progress of the project and how it can be used as a means of demonstrating to the customer where the project is headed and how much there is left to go.

Bear in mind that the number of sprints in a project should be dictated by the work to be done itself and the time you have available to do it in. So, this is why the planning process, just like the entire project itself, should be a collaborative effort that fosters communication and leads to effective decisions based on everyone's collective experience and insight.

At the end of the day, the lifecycle of a Scrum project is based on the team's ability to stay on track. This is why the only truly rigid aspect of Scrum is the respect to the overall time allotted to each task. This discipline enables Scrum teams to meet their deadlines on a consistent basis.

Chapter 4: Roles in Scrum and Responsibilities

In the previous chapter, we talked about what a Scrum sprint is in great depth and how you put your first Scrum project together. In addition, we focused on the ins and outs of selecting your Scrum team. As such, this discussion was intended to get your mind working on how you can implement Scrum in your organization.

In this chapter, we will focus specifically on the roles contained within a Scrum project. We have already touched upon each one of these roles, though the time has come to be far more specific since each one of the players on a Scrum team has a specific role which they must fulfill. Furthermore, we will have a much closer look at what type of criteria will go into selecting each one of the team members.

Where to Find Qualified Players

Finding qualified Scrum practitioners isn't as easy as you might think. While Scrum has gained considerable popularity in recent years, qualified Scrum practitioners aren't quite as easy to find. The reason for this is that there is still some lack of knowledge and understanding of the value of Scrum and project management as a whole.

Nevertheless, more and more companies are trying their best to recruit talent which has received some type of Scrum training. Also, companies may be looking to hire individuals who have taken Scrum training. This is especially true in the software and IT industries.

When you, and your organization, decide to go all-in on Scrum, it's often a good idea to build a culture of Scrum from within, that is, train current staff in the ways of Scrum. This can be a good way to foster team building and encourage your staff to work as a team in a collaborative manner. Most importantly, you're initiating the mindset transition from a traditional approach of doing business to a more Agile approach.

Thus, implementing Scrum in your organization leaves you with two options: either bringing in someone external who can get started with Scrum in your organization, or train your current staff in the ways of Agile. Please bear in mind that training your staff can be a way in which your organization can reward and motivate its staff in order to improve their skills and knowledge.

One way of training your staff without breaking the bank is through hiring an Agile Coach. An Agile Coach can help your staff learn the ways of Agile and Scrum in such a way that your organization and staff can shift their mindset to an Agile mindset.

The Agile Mindset

When an organization makes the decision to go Agile, the biggest challenge they face is shifting from a traditional mindset to an Agile one. This shift in mentality is a means of changing focus to a customer-centered approach in which embracing change is the primary focus.

This can prove to be both scary and even overwhelming to some folks.

Embracing change is not easy for many individuals and organizations. When organizations go down this road, individuals become closer-knit and more resilient. This resiliency makes organizations more adaptable and increasingly confident in operating within a dynamic environment.

In a way, an Agile mindset is about selling the idea to both staff and customers that change is to be embraced even when there is very little certainty about what might happen at the end of the project. While this approach does not imply improvising, it does mean that organizations need to think on their feet in order to produce the results that will get customers what they are looking to achieve.

That being said, Agile considers the following traits are prerequisites for Scrum practitioners:

- Positive attitude
- Willingness to learn
- Desire to serve others
- Provide value at all times
- Willingness to change
- Search for continuous improvement

While these characteristics are not exhaustive, they are some of the most common prerequisite characteristics that individuals need in order to embrace the Agile mindset. Of course, this isn't a cookie-cutter approach. However, the main aspect of this list is about making sure that potential Scrum practitioners have the willingness to embrace this change in mindset.

It should be noted that there are folks who may not be willing to embrace the Agile mindset. And they are in the right to choose to act the way they see fit. However, in order for Scrum to be effectively implemented, all team members need to be all-in in this mentality.

So, if you are looking to train your team, it's best to make sure that everyone is willing to go through the rigors that entail becoming a quality Scrum practitioner.

The Main Roles in Scrum

Throughout the book, we have highlighted the three main roles in Scrum: The Product Owner, Scrum Master, and Development Team. The actual number of players on a Scrum team will depend on the size and the scope of the project. Nevertheless, a standard project will require one Product Owner, one Scrum Master, and a Development Team that may consist of about 4 to 6 members.

It is not recommended to have a number greater than 6 members on a Development Team, nor is it advisable to have a number lower than 4. 4 members seems to be the ideal number as it is an even amount and provides the possibility of working in pairs.

If you happen to choose and odd-numbered Development Team, for instance, 5 members, there might be some discomfort since the team may not be able to break into pairs, or even may have difficulty in dividing up work. In addition, having an even-numbered Development Team provides asymmetry in the way the work can be divided and distributed.

Also, each Scrum project must have a Product Owner and Scrum Master. It is not recommended that to have one person play both roles as this could lead to a potential conflict in the way this individual may relate to both the customer and the Development Team. Since the Scrum Master's role is mostly about serving the Development Team, doubling up as a Product Owner may lead to one individual to be overloaded between the requests from both the customer and the Scrum Master.

In a way, the Product Owner should be on the customer's side. The reason for having this attitude is due to the fact that the Product Owner serves as a buffer between both the customer and the Development Team. This is why doubling up as Product Owner, and Scrum Master may lead this individual to take on too much especially if the project has a high degree of uncertainty and pressure due to time constraints.

With that being said, let's take a closer look at how each role plays out in greater detail.

Scrum Product Owner

The Scrum Product Owner is known as the "voice of the customer." As such, serving as the voice of the customer entails being on the "customer's side." What this means is that the Product Owner is the one who takes on the role of being a project lead without actually being the boss.

This is a very important shift considering that traditional project management methods espouse a "project manager" who is the boss and leader of the project. The project manager is the person who is responsible for the outcomes of the project but is also invested with all of the authority to make the project work.

In the case of the Product Owner, the Product Owner is not "the boss" since the Product Owner is in charge of making sure that all parties are working in unison. Considering that the Product Owner is not the boss of the project, the responsibility for the project's outcomes are not completely placed on the Product Owner's shoulders. This is a very important aspect to consider since the responsibility of the project can be distributed over the entire team and not just on one person.

Of course, if the responsibility for the project is distributed evenly among all members, then the credit for the project is also distributed evenly among all members. Therefore, the entire Scrum team needs to be on the same page. That is why all members of a Scrum team need to be willing to commit to this mindset. If there is any member that is not committed to this approach, then the project may encounter headwinds from within.

The Product Owner is the first member that should come on board for every new project.

But, where does the Product Owner come from?

Well, every project needs to have a project sponsor. The project sponsor is the main interested party in getting the project off the ground.

Earlier, I used the example of a company that is looking to change its benefits scheme. In that case, the CEO brought the need for a new benefit scheme to the Board of the company so that the project initiative may be authorized.

In this example, the CEO is the project sponsor as it was their initiative. Consequently, the CEO decided to ask the Human Resources Manager of the company to find a qualified individual who could act as a project lead. Since the project was conceived under the Agile framework, the project lead is not the Product Owner. The CEO continues to be the project sponsor while the Human Resources Manager, the person who hired the Product Owner, ends up becoming the customer.

So, why should the Human Resources Manager become the customer and not the CEO?

The CEO has a personal stake in this project. It was the CEO who advocated for the project to be done. This could entail a personal conviction for the project's realization. Therefore, the CEO would not be an objective party in the development of the project.

However, the Human Resources Manager may not have a personal stake in the project. This manager might be the one in charge of running the company's benefits scheme. So, they would be interested in making sure the project is done properly and also understands what the company's staff needs and demands from a good benefits scheme.

So, the Human Resources Manager becomes the customer while the Product Owner is now the focal point of the project. As such, the Product Owner is in charge of putting the project team together. This opens up an interesting point: the customer has no bearing on who is chosen to be on the Scrum team, though they may have some input as to the type of players they are looking from. After all, the customer is paying for the project. However, the customer needs to understand that their direct involvement in the project may end up doing more harm than good if it is not handled proactively and positively.

Ideally, the Product Owner should be an experienced Scrum practitioner even if they are not entirely familiar with the subject matter. The Scrum Product Owner needs to be a great negotiator and coordinator so that all of the activities which are carried out throughout the lifecycle of the project. Consequently, the Scrum Product Owner must be involved in the project from the beginning till the end even if the Product Owner is not directly involved in the actual development of the product.

One important word of caution for project sponsors: the first step toward launching any Scrum-based project is finding the Product Owner. Even if the project sponsor already has a potential team in place, the Product Owner needs to be in synch with the Scrum Master and Development Team. Therefore, choosing the Scrum Master or Development Team ahead of the Product Owner may lead to friction among all members. So, even if the project sponsor has people in mind, this decision may be discussed with the Product Owner, but it is the Product Owner's ultimate decision on who to include in the project team.

Also, if the project sponsor is bent on deciding who is on the team, then Scrum might not be the best approach. Since this attitude implies a more hierarchical approach, then a traditional project management approach may be more suited to this attitude. That way, the project sponsor can take the lead and let everyone else around them follow orders.

This is why Scrum is about working in a collaborative environment with a flat organizational structure. This breeds empowerment and allows Scrum team members to flex their muscles in search of a creative solution to the problems being addressed.

The Scrum Master

As I have stated earlier, the reason why the Scrum Master is called a "master" is not because of their domain over the team, but rather, it is due to their mastery of the Scrum methodology. This implies that the Scrum Master needs to be well-versed in Agile methodologies focusing specifically on Scrum. In addition, the Scrum Master should have a good level of knowledge on the project's subject matter. Therefore, the Scrum Master needs to be a well-rounded individual.

Unlike the Product Owner, who doesn't need to be well-versed in the project's subject matter, the Scrum Master needs to be involved in all technical aspects of the solution being required. The main reason for this is that the Scrum Master needs to clearly articulate the customer's vision, as expressed by the Product Owner, into the language that the Development Team can understand.

Since the Scrum Master is a subservient leader, their role is focused on helping the

Development Team get the most out of the resources they have available while maximizing the results obtained during each sprint. This means that the Scrum Master is not there to "lead" anybody, but rather, just be the figurehead which can provide the necessary guidance when the team requires it.

Bear in mind that the Development Team should be self-organizing. So, that means that the Development Team should be able to work out everything they need to work out on their own. However, there are times when the Development Team may need a referee to sort out the way things should be conducted. As such, the Scrum Master doesn't have to be "right" but should be able to provide proper guidance.

In the cases in which there is any type of dispute as to the proper application of Scrum methodology, then the final decision falls on the Product Owner. It is the Product Owner who needs to provide proper guidance on the way the project is to be conducted. Again, this isn't about being right, but it's about having clear judgment as to how the methodology should be applied.

Moreover, the Scrum Master is in charge of making sure that the general guidelines of the sprint are being followed. For instance, the Scrum Master leads the Daily Standup Meeting and is in charge of going over the Sprint Burndown Chart. This is why it is required for the Scrum Master to be involved with the Development Team on a daily basis. While it isn't necessary for the Scrum Master to be sitting in the same room looking over everyone's shoulder to see what they are doing, it is a good idea for the Scrum Master to check in regularly to keep tabs on the work that is being done. The entire point of doing that is to make sure that if any potential issues arise, these can be caught in time.

The Scrum Master would ideally be someone who is experienced in Scrum while having a good working knowledge of the subject matter pertaining to the project.

So, assuming the previous example of the benefits scheme, the Scrum Master would not only be experienced in Scrum itself but would also have a working knowledge of payroll matters, compensation, benefits, finance, and any other applicable fields. As you can see, the Scrum Master is indeed a very well-rounded person that can provide insights into the actual subject matter but can also provide the necessary guidance to ensure that the project is conducted in the proper fashion.

If the Scrum Master isn't as experienced or is just starting out in this role, then the Product Owner may have to become more involved in working with the Scrum Master but not the Development Team. This would entail having more frequent meetings and phone calls just to check in with what's going on. In that regard, the Scrum Master may rely a lot more on the Product Owner for guidance and direction especially when there are methodological issues that need to be addressed.

In that regard, the Product Owner becomes a type of coach for the Scrum Master who then "coaches" the Development Team. However, when the Product Owner is under pressure, or may not be as experienced in the rigors of Scrum, then the project sponsor might consider bringing in an Agile Coach.

The Role of the Agile Coach

Earlier, we discussed who the Agile coach was and what they do within a Scrum project. As such, the Agile Coach is not a team member since the role of the Agile Coach is exists only when needed. What the Agile Coach does is provide definitive guidance on the way the project is to be conducted. Thus, the Agile Coach needs to be a veteran leader who has been involved with Scrum for a given period of time.

The Agile Coach can be an individual consultant, or perhaps a consultancy firm that provides these services. In the case that the Scrum team is comprised of members who work for the organization, then the Agile Coach needs to be external. This is important in ensuring the objectivity and impartial nature of the Agile Coach. If the Agile Coach is not objective, then what might happen is that an Agile Coach from within the organization may end up having a personal stake in the project. Therefore, this may lead to some bias in the way the project is applied.

In addition, an internal Agile Coach may be a bit reluctant to point out any shortcoming and inefficiencies out of concern for negatively affecting colleagues. As such, an independent Agile Coach can provide guidance and correct potential issues in the application of the methodology without really having to worry about stepping on any toes.

It should also be noted that the Agile Coach is not there to provide guidance on the way the project's outputs are being produced. In fact, the Agile Coach is limited to being a consultant in the project's methodology itself and not the product being produced.

So, let's assume that the Development Team has questions about the legality of a compensation scheme that they are working on. This would not be the competency of the Agile Coach, but rather, it would be the competency of legal counsel.

In that case, the Scrum Master may request the Product Owner to seek proper legal counsel and set up a meeting to discuss their questions. These consultations would ideally be coordinated by the Product Owner. Then, the Scrum Master may also be a part of the meetings in order to get the right idea on what the legal ramifications of the new compensation scheme would be.

After the consultation, the Scrum Master would go back to the Development Team and address any questions they may have. Since the Scrum Master has a working knowledge on the subject matter, they would be qualified to address the team on the subject. The Product Owner would just sit in the wings observing that the Scrum Master has a handle on the situation.

In the worst of cases, the Development Team may have to meet with the legal counsel in order to hear their opinion. While this may not be detrimental to the team in any way, it may temporarily put a halt to the team's work. That is why the ideal course of action would be to have the Scrum Master gain all the information needed while the team continues to work. As such, the Scrum Master's job, in this case, is in the background.

The Development Team

Last, but certainly not least, the Development Team is the main the component of the team. When the Product Owner and Scrum Master have agreed on all of the terms of the project, such as the Project Charter and user stories (unless being developed by the entire team), then the Development Team can be put into place.

Assuming that the team is entirely new, the Product Owner and the Scrum Master would have to make sure that they are qualified individuals who share the values of the Agile mindset. Now, if they have already worked in the past and have achieved a good degree of affinity, then much of this process would be reduced.

The members of the Development Team should all have had at least some training and exposure to Scrum while not necessarily being experts on Agile methodology. Ideally, they would be certified in Scrum development, though this may not necessarily be a deal breaker.

Members of the Development Team should also have a working knowledge of the subject matters on which the project is based. In the example of the benefits scheme, the Development Team could be a group of accountants who are experienced in compensations and benefits. Thus, a group of four accountants could be tasked with the development of the project.

For example, one individual might be in charge of going over the company's payroll history in order to determine the costs and benefits of the current benefits scheme. Another member might be in charge of putting together a list of viable benefits to be included in the new scheme. Another member might be in charge of calculating how much each of the individual benefits would save/cost the company while the fourth member of the team might be in charge of reviewing the company's balance sheet and cash flow statement to determine how much the company can reasonably spend.

As you can see, these activities all require technical knowledge in the field of accounting and finance. Since the Development Team members may not be very experienced with Scrum, the Scrum Master would be "holding their hand" at the beginning of the first sprint while the Development Team gains a good level of comfort with the way the project is to be conducted.

At the end of the first sprint, the deliverable from the Development Team could be a solid proposal for the company's Board to vote on. This proposal would contain a series of recommendations to be presented so that the directors can decide which benefits to keep and which ones would not be appropriate for their vision of the company.

Therefore, one of the acceptance criteria might be to have cost-effective benefits that the company doesn't have to actually pay out in monetary terms but could be offered to staff as a perk for working for the company.

Once the Board votes, they choose which initiatives to approve and which ones to axe. Then, the Product Owner meets with the Human Resources Manager and gets a series of change requests based on the appreciation of the company's Board. The Product Owner then talks with the Scrum Master to determine how these changes can affect the work already planned.

The change request is discussed at the next Sprint Planning Meeting. The Development Team can then get down to work and implement the final recommendations made by the board. As such, the second sprint would be to produce the final document which contains the company's new benefits scheme. This final draft of the document would constitute the final output of the project.

Then, the document is formally presented to the Board by means of a presentation conducted by the entire team. The Product Owner and Scrum Master are on hand to supervise what the Development Team has to say to the Board. The Human Resources Manager officially acts as the customer while the CEO and the Board are the relevant stakeholders.

The final draft is then approved, and the final product is officially accepted by the client. This marks the end of the project.

Do you recall that this project had 8 weeks to be completed? So, we decided to break it down into two, four-week sprints. And now, the project is officially at a close.

The remaining activities would be to have the Sprint Retrospect Meeting in which the entire team reflects on how the last sprint went and what could have been better.

Finally, there is a Project Retrospect Meeting in which the project is officially wrapped up. This meeting might end up being more social than work-related, but it is essential in order to bring the project to a formal close.

The Product Owner would be in charge of cleaning up the office after the Development Team has been disbanded and everyone goes their separate ways.

In the event that the members were part of the company itself, then they would go back to their usual jobs. In the case that the Development Team were all external consultants, then they would move on to other projects, either as a team or as individual members.

The Product Owner would be in charge of wrapping up the final details with the customer while the Scrum Master may still be on board for a bit longer in order to handle any loose ends with the documentation pertaining to the project.

With the conclusion of the project, the final deliverable is implemented by the customer and the story comes to an end.

Now, you might be asking yourself: wait a minute, what about the testing of the scheme?

Well, that is something that we are going to tackle in the next chapter.

Chapter 5: Metrics in Scrum

One of the core tenets of effective project management is producing metrics that can track the progress of a project. Without a solid, quantitative measurement of project performance, it is nearly impossible to accurately measure how effective the project actually is. In fact, offering a qualitative measure of the effectiveness of a project provides a very limited scope of just how well the project is doing.

Consequently, it is vital that project leaders develop a series of indicators which can be used to determine the progress of the project and verify how well the results of the project have been achieved. Based on that premise, Scrum, just like any other project management methodology out there, seeks to use indicators, formally known as Key

Performance Indicators (or KPIs) to measure the success of the project and track its output.

In this chapter, we will be looking at the KPIs which can be used to track project development in order to ensure that the outputs established at the outset of the project are met.

Who is in Charge of Tracking KPIs?

The first point that needs to be taken into consideration is: who is in charge of tracking KPIs?

The measurement of overall project success and progress is a collaborative effort, just like everything else in Scrum. The Product Owner is in charge of the overall reporting process, especially when reporting to the customer and other stakeholders on the progress of the project.

In addition, the Scrum Master is in charge of compiling the relevant information that is used to generate the indicators. For instance, this refers to tracking the results of individual Sprint Tasks which build up to the Product Backlog items.

The Development Team is also in charge of tracking their own progress such as the number of hours that have been worked and which are remaining in the sprint, the progress they have made in their individual tasks in addition to any bugs or problems encountered in the testing portion of the deliverables.

It should be noted that even if the Product Owner is in charge of compiling the KPIs for the project, this does not mean that the Product Owner has the authority to "supervise" the project. Please keep in mind that Scrum espouses a concept of transparency and mutual accountability. What this means is that everyone is in charge of tracking the progress of the project and not just the Product Owner.

Also, the Scrum Master is just keeping track of the tasks being completed in such a way that if there are issues that arise within the project itself, the Development Team has the opportunity to bring them up at the next available time which would be the Daily Standup Meeting.

Consequently, there is no officially tracker or supervisor. Everyone is in charge of keeping tabs on everyone. If there should ever be any disciplinary issues, the team, as a whole, has the responsibility and the authority to deal with the issue among themselves. This is one of the most important features of self-organizing teams.

Scrum Metrics and KPIs

The metrics used in Scrum are part of the broader group of Agile KPIs. These metrics serve as the parameters by which the progress of the project is measured in an objective and quantitative manner. Now, there are other metrics and methodologies which could come into play such as combining a Scrum project with Six Sigma or the use of Kanban metrics which track workflow.

The fact of the matter is that there is a wide range of metrics which could be used, and all depend on the project itself. As such, Scrum practitioners quickly come to realize that no two projects are the same and they may all end up requiring different metrics to measure their output.

Nevertheless, there are three broad types of metrics which can be used to generate KPIs.

• **Measuring deliverables**. These metrics measure the output of the Scrum team and the amount of value being provided to customers. This measurement can be in terms of time saved, cost reduction, increased sales, or any other type of impact the project has had on the customer. Also, deliverables may be measured in terms of their individual functionalities. This refers to the specific characteristics of the project and how it can be tracked to ensure that the final product does what it's supposed to do.

- **Measuring effectiveness**. These metrics measure the overall effectiveness and success of the Scrum team. There is a myriad of metrics here. Some that stand out are Return on Investment (ROI), time to market, and so on. These metrics focus on the impact that the Scrum team's actions had on the business itself, or even the industry.

- **Measuring the Scrum team**. These metrics look to determine the overall health of the team in terms of member satisfaction, turnover, and even attrition. This measurement allows the Scrum Master and Product Owner to determine if the way the project is being handled is appropriate if the tempo is moving too fast, or if there are any other considerations which must be taken into account.

The three broad categories of metrics described above are to provide a sense of what the Scrum team should be producing, where they stand in terms of the overall progress of the project and if there are any potential issues which could be caught ahead of time and dealt with in a proactive manner.

Therefore, it is up to the Product Owner to help the Scrum Master determine if the team is firing on all cylinders or if there are any issues within the team that need to be addressed at once.

In addition, it's important for the Product Owner to be aware of how metrics from other disciplines, such as Six Sigma, could potentially help the Development Team, and any other stakeholder, gain a better perspective of how well the project is doing. Ultimately, the success of the project is measured in the customer's satisfaction and the overall achievement of the project's aim. Moreover, the success of a project is measured by the amount of value that was ultimately delivered to the customer as a result of the deliverables.

Now, let's dig deeper into the specifics of each of the three broad categories we have described above.

Metrics Used to Measure Deliverables

This is the first category that we are going to take a look at. In it, you will find a series of metrics used to measure the overall success of the deliverables being provided to the customer. As such, the customers, as well as, all project stakeholders will have the opportunity to see just how well the deliverables are performing based on the project's individual characteristics.

These KPIs are a measure of how well the Scrum team has been able to deliver value to its customers and thereby accomplish the aims of the project. This measure of customer satisfaction enables the Scrum team to see if they are heading in the right direction, or if there is a need to make adjustments.

It should also be noted that since there is always partial delivery of outputs, it is possible to see how outputs are performing at the end of each sprint. This will enable the Scrum team to make any adjustments based on the feedback received during the Sprint Review Meeting.

Sprint Goal Success

The Sprint Goal Success is an Agile metric adapted specifically to fit the Scrum framework. This metric enables the Scrum team to determine if the overall result of the sprint was successful. In order to generate this metric, three basic questions need to be answered:

- What is the point of the sprint?
- What can we do to achieve the sprint goal?
- How can we tell we have achieved the goal?

The answers to these three questions should be able to guide you in determining if the overall result of the sprint was successful, or not.

So, the first question, "what is the point of the sprint?" refers to the sprint's main objective, that is, what is the overall goal of the sprint?

The answer could be something as simple as, "provide a functioning demo version of the software." This means that at the end of the sprint, the Scrum team should be able to have a fully-functioning demo version for the customer to evaluate.

The second question, "what can we do to achieve the sprint goal?" refers to the actions and resources that need to be combined in order to determine if the goal is reachable, or not. These goals can be taken from the Product Backlog and put into practice in each sprint through the Sprint tasks determined at the outset of the sprint during the Sprint Planning Meeting.

The third question, "how can we tell we have achieved the goal?" refers to finding an objective measure that can determine if the goal was met. If it was, then the Sprint Retrospective Meeting can capture the successful actions implemented. If the goal was partially met, or if the team failed to meet, then the very same Sprint Retrospective Meeting can be used to determine what went wrong and how it can be improved.

Ultimately, the criteria which can be used to determine if the sprint has been successful to compare the outputs based on the acceptance criteria. If the outputs comply with the acceptance criteria, then there is a good chance the customer will be satisfied even if the request changes. However, if the acceptance criteria are not reflected in the output, then the Development Team needs to go back and see how they can get back up to speed.

Escaped Defects

This metric tracks the number of bugs that the Development Team encountered during the development of the product. This particular metric is ideal for tracking those products which are reliant on testing in order to make sure it works well.

This metric can be used in manufacturing, software development, pharma, and even food production. If you look at it those terms, you can put Scrum to use in any field in which defects are tracked. The big difference between Scrum and other manufacturing systems such as Total Quality is that you are not waiting till the end of the production cycle to see where the defects are. With Scrum, you can gauge how many errors are popping during the manufacturing phase. Therefore, you will be able to determine if there are corrections that need to be made.

Defect Density

And, on the subject of defects, the Defect Density metric measures how many defects were found per unit of production. In the case of software, for instance, you could track the number of mistakes per lines of code. In manufacturing, you could track the number of mistakes per thousand units of production. The measurements may vary, but the concept is the same. As such, it's important to keep track of this measurement as it is vital to ensure that you have the right number of defects.

Team Velocity

This is a more Scrum-like measure. In essence, team velocity is measured by the number of user stories completed in a sprint, or the amount of Product Backlog items finalized.

Now, this metric is not an exact metric in the sense that some sprints may yield the completion of a significant number of products while other sprints may produce a very limited number. This all depends on the actual work breakdown that has been determined at the outset of the sprint.

Nevertheless, it is a useful measurement in tracking the actual work that the Development Team is achieving per sprint. However, it might be unfair to compare one sprint with another since conditions may be changing and the dynamics of the project may require one set of tasks over another. Thus, this may lead the team to produce a high number of outputs in one sprint while the remaining number of sprints may yield a lower amount of outputs.

At the end of the day, the team serves as a means of tracking the amount of work being done. As the completed work piles up, the Scrum team can see the success of their actions.

A word of caution though: in the case where there are multiple Scrum teams, it's important to avoid the sure of team velocity as a means of comparing team performance. Unless you have multiple teams completing the exact same tasks (which would be pointless) you would not have an "apples to apples" comparison. This means that while one team is apparently getting more work done than other teams, this measurement is not fair since each team is working on completely different tasks. As such, this is a flawed metric in terms of using it as a comparison among teams.

Sprint Burndown

The Sprint Burndown is a measure in which the sprint's total working hours are divided by the number of work days available.

Let's assume that a Scrum team has four weeks to complete a sprint. Then, let's assume they are working 8 hours a day over a 5-day week, that's 20 work days at a clip of 160 total hours of work.

This means that each day, 8 hours will tick off the Burndown Chart. If the team is humming along, there may be no need to work overtime. However, it could be that the Development Team has encountered issues and needs to put in a few extra hours. This would be reflected in the number of hours the team is working on a daily basis.

Consequently, you can chart the team's work by generating a bar graph representing the number of hours worked per day. The trend line for the chart would gradually wind down to zero as the number of hours run out.

The Sprint Burndown Chart serves as a graphic organizer in which the team can see where they are heading in terms of the remaining hours in the sprint versus the amount of work remaining. It should be said that if everything is humming along perfectly and the work assigned to that sprint takes less time than anticipated, the leftover time is automatically assigned to testing. That way, no time is wasted.

Measuring Effectiveness

The next set of metrics are used to measure how successful the Scrum team has been in achieving the business goals set forth the outset of the project and in each sprint. Thus, the Scrum team can see how effective they have been in generating value to the customer and to the team itself.

Time to Market

This metric tracks the amount of time the Scrum project actually takes before the product begins to generate income for the customer. So, this would be the number of sprints it would take the Scrum team before the final product is officially released and begins to generate income for the customer.

Let's consider a software release such as a video game. The Scrum team has determined that it would take four, four-week sprints before the Scrum team would have a demo version available for testing. At this point, the game would not be up for sale yet, but the advance speculation would provide the customer with some traction. As such, value is being created without actually being up for sale.

When the video game is fully operational and ready to generate income, then the Scrum team will have the final release of the product to the customer. At this point, the customer can begin to generate income off the product's final release.

This measure is also depending on the Scrum team's alpha and beta testing procedures. It could be that beta testing may take up an entire sprint since the product itself is so extensive. And once beta testing is complete, the product may enter the market under alpha testing guidelines. As such, this may represent another full sprint while the final bugs are worked out for the product.

As you can see, time to market becomes more and more critical as the project grows in size and scope. Therefore, it's crucial for the Scrum team to set realistic timelines so that the customer can be aware of the amount of the time the project will need before the final product is released.

Return on Investment (ROI)

This metric can be used on both sides of the ball.

For the Scrum team, their work generates an income to the company which has employed them to deliver the service to the customer. As such, the ROI for the company employing the Scrum team may be measured in terms of the costs associated with each sprint versus what the customer has actually paid for the services rendered.

This is fairly straightforward, and the Scrum team would most likely generate costs in terms of wages, equipment, and other materials used to produce the final product for the customer. Since the Scrum team may be employed by a company external to the customer, this external company, perhaps a consulting firm would have to make an upfront investment in equipment and training in order to get the Scrum team fully operational.

On the customer's side, the customer will measure the expense that arose from the actual payment of the services rendered by the Scrum team. This payment could be calculated and agreed upon in a number of ways. At the end of the day, the customer hopes to generate much more income as compared to the expense it incurred in during the production of the project's outputs.

The easiest way to breakdown costing for a Scrum project is per sprint. Since each sprint may have very different activities attached to them, the Scrum team may reduce or increase costs depending on the actions that are done.

Ultimately, the Product Owner and Scrum Master need to keep close track of the expenses incurred by the Development Team. In traditional project management approaches, one of the key elements in the planning phase is the development of a project budget.

In Scrum, since less documentation is favored, the Product Owner should be encouraged to have a means of tracking expenses such as a solid spreadsheet, which can keep tabs on the money being spent on project-related items. The worst thing that a project team can do is completely disregard their costs. So, it certainly pays to keep track of this metric.

Capital Redeployment

This is a very tricky subject.

At the outset of the project, the Product Owner needs to determine what capital equipment is going to be needed in order to carry out the tasks needed to produce the final output for the project.

In that regard, the Product Owner needs to see if the current capital equipment, such as computers, machines, or any other type of equipment can handle the demands of the project. Otherwise, the Scrum team may need to invest in new equipment in order to get the job done effectively. When there are acquisitions in capital equipment at the outset of the project, this is called "capital deployment."

However, what happens if there is a need to acquire more equipment mid-way through the project?

This is the case of "capital redeployment."

One consideration might be the acquisition of new equipment. Since it is likely that the new equipment may not be fully used up by the end of the project, it could still serve for a future project. Nevertheless, the cost of the equipment needs to be contrasted versus the reaming work to be done. When the cost of the new equipment exceeds the economic value remaining in the project, then this situation of "capital redeployment" makes no sense for the Scrum team.

Consider this situation:

About 60% of the project has already been completed. Consequently, the customer has already paid more than half of their share in the project. With about 40% of the work remaining, the Scrum team has determined that there is the need to acquire new computer systems in order to finish the remaining amount of work.

Now, for the sake of simplicity, let's assume that the customer owes the Scrum team $1,000. The cost of the brand-new equipment is $750. The Product Owner has determined that this would essentially zap any profits the Scrum team could make. Therefore, another option needs to be considered.

In the end, the Product Owner has decided that refurbished equipment would be more suitable given the amount of time remaining in the project. Consequently, the acquisition of brand-new equipment does not make sense for the Scrum team. Such a situation may have been avoided in a carefully-planned project, but there are always unforeseen events. For instance, the customer has put in change requests that forced the Scrum team to expand the scope of the project and hire new developers. So, it is certainly worth taking this into consideration.

Customer Satisfaction

The Scrum team's biggest concern is having a satisfied customer. Now, in the case of a project, customer satisfaction essentially means that the guy who's paying needs to be happy with the product and not the actual users.

Nevertheless, it's important for the Scrum team to track what the users have to say about the product. In this case, customer satisfaction can be measured during the beta testing phase. For instance, beta testers can fill out a short questionnaire following their experience with the product.

This questionnaire can have easily measurable metrics such as "like," star ratings, recommendations, or even abstract measurements such as asking users how much they would be willing to pay for a product such as this one.

Once the product is released, the Scrum team, most notably the Product Owner, may choose to hold some type of customer satisfaction review. This would enable the project stakeholders to determine how well the product met the expectations of the customer and the users. They may lead to another project in which bugs and kinks are worked out, or an alpha testing sprint that would officially bring the project to a close even after the product has reached the hands of the users.

Customer satisfaction can be contrasted with metrics such as ROI in order to visualize just how effective the project was in the end. Ultimately, this measurement would provide the stakeholders with a clear vision of what the product is able to do moving forward.

Monitoring the Scrum Team

These metrics are used to gauge the health of the Scrum team.

At the outset of this book, we mentioned how important people were over processes and equipment. And it goes without saying that the most important people in a Scrum project are the members of the Development Team. Without them, none of the work would be possible to do no matter how intelligent and talented the Product Owner and Scrum Master may be.

So, these metrics can be used to track the overall performance of the team and determine how well they are doing as a team, independent of their outputs.

Using Meetings to Gauge Health

The Daily Standup Meetings and the Sprint Retrospective Meetings are used to reflect on the daily tasks being conducted, as well as, the tasks achieved during the previous sprint.

It is during these meetings that the Product Owner and the Scrum Master can see just how well the team is performing. These meetings are a great way for the Scrum Master to pick up on potential issues within the team itself. Perhaps the team is encountering a difficulty which can be addressed early and well before it festers into something completely detrimental to the Scrum team's performance.

Also, the Scrum Master may pick up on potential issues which the Product Owner can bring up with the customer in order to figure out how to proactively deal with them. As such, meetings should be productive in such a way that the Development Team can use that time to generate the information that the Scrum Master and the Product Owner will need in order to fine-tune the processes being put into place.

Furthermore, the Scrum team needs to maintain open lines of communication at all time. Therefore, the Scrum team needs to be able to address issues within the team, given its self-organizing nature, without having to resort to additional intervention from the Scrum Master or the Product Owner.

Team Satisfaction

This is a hard one to track.

On the one hand, you could take your team member's word for it and take their comments at face value. So, if they say they are doing well, you could take that a face value and decide they are feeling fine. Likewise, if the team says things are not going well, you can take that at face value and determine what needs to be done in order to avoid future issues.

Now, you could find a more systematic approach, such as a reporting system in which team members can track how they feel on a daily basis by depositing smiley or sad faces in a box before they go home for the day. The Scrum Master can see how many smiley or sad faces are deposited at the end of each day. Since this is a perfectly anonymous task, Development Team members may feel compelled to be honest. Of course, there will come a time when they will have to indicate what's getting to them. But that can be part of one-on-one talks between the Scrum Master and individual team members.

It should be noted that satisfaction is something subjective. And, most Development Team members may simply feel overwhelmed by the tempo of the project or may feel uncomfortable especially if they are new to Scrum. So, encouraging constant communication at all times is vital to a healthy project.

Staff Turnover

We briefly touched on this subject earlier. There is a very real possibility that you may have to find replacements for team members mid-sprint. Of course, you would like to have a situation in which team members don't flake out in the middle of a sprint, but if it does happen, then you would be hard pressed to find a replacement.

Some Scrum teams like to have a "bench." This would mean a five-member squad when, in reality, four members are needed. But the fifth member is there to replace anyone who leaves. That will allow the team to cope with the work remaining as opposed to having a four-member team and the suddenly being shorthanded with three or even two members.

Turnover is a measure of how well the team is feeling. So, if you have a higher rate of turnover, then the team is not feeling well. If there is little turnover, then you can feel confident that the Development Team is doing just fine.

Final Considerations

When looking at metrics in a Scrum project, you must have a clear vision of which elements you can track objectively, and which ones would be tracked in a more subjective manner. Ideally, you would be able to track everything with statistical and numerical data in such a way that you could generate reliable numbers.

As such, great care needs to be taken in avoiding the use of the wrong type of metrics. When the wrong metrics are used, the information obtained may be misleading and thereby cause you to make inappropriate decisions. So, it certainly pays to do your homework on what metrics you could use in order to keep adequate track of your project.

I would greatly encourage you to look at comparable projects, whenever possible, to see which metrics you put into practice so that you can get a better understanding of how you can measure your team's performance.

Furthermore, using the right metrics to measure customer satisfaction will enable you to determine how effective the project was. At the end of the day, customer satisfaction is the ultimate measure of success for any Scrum project.

Chapter 6: Applications of Scrum

We are beginning to come to the stretch drive of this book. But there is still lots more to discuss.

In this chapter, we will be looking at the applications of Scrum. That is, we will be discussing how and where Scrum can be applied. This will give you a broader perspective on how Scrum is not just limited to software development. Since Scrum has cross-cutting applications, it's definitely worth jumping into a deeper discussion on how Scrum can be applied to your organization.

Born out of Software Development

When Agile was developed, traditional project management methodologies had been unable to address the issues pertaining to dynamic and ever-changing environments. This led project managers to seek alternatives that would embrace change and help software developers find the right way in which they could address these dynamics while making the most out of the current project management techniques available.

Out of this need, approaches such as Extreme Programming allowed developers to find a host of principles which could better address the circumstances they face as developers in a volatility environment.

Since 2001, the Agile movement has led to the emergence of Scrum as a viable methodology which can provide developers a series of steps and procedures in order to create a project framework conducive to getting results.

Given that we have already covered the history of Scrum; it's worth mentioning at this point that the software industry is the most common place where Scrum can be found in action. But it is not the only place in which Scrum can be implemented. In fact, Scrum can be implemented in any type of industry and business.

It Starts with the Agile Mindset

Throughout the book, we have talked about the Agile mindset.

In that regard, the Agile mindset is all about putting people first. In this case, the people that go first are the customer and the individual team members.

When you move away from getting results based on the cold metrics that are just numbers on a page to an approach where success is measured by the success of individuals, then you are setting yourself up for a successful run at each project.

One of the most crucial success factors in Scrum is determining if team members have the right mindset. This may imply having to "sell" individuals on the merits of Scrum especially if they have been exposed to other project management methodologies which espouse more rigid principles.

The fact of the matter is that anyone who is truly dedicated to providing the best value at all times will quickly see the merits of Scrum for what they are. As long as team members are willing to focus on delivering value at all times, and not just "getting the job done," then you can be sure that you will be successful in the long run.

A Cross-Cutting Approach

Scrum has a cross-cutting approach in the sense that it can be applied to virtually any industry and business out there. This is something which is important to take into account as project management is a diverse field.

Given that there is no, one methodology which is "perfect," new approaches are consistently being developed. As such, each approach attempts to tackle the gaps that other approaches have failed to address, either due to obsolescence or due to inadequacy on the part of their practitioners.

In any event, Scrum can be implemented in just about every walk of life. Increasingly, more and more industries are getting their staff Scrum certified so that they can tackle project management, and daily tasks, within an Agile environment.

Consequently, being "Agile" means being able to trim away the fat from your organization and focusing on getting results rather than sounding smart. In fact, you will sound even smarter when you are able to deliver on your promises as opposed to having to justify your team as to why your objectives were not met.

In this regard, you have the power to choose Scrum as a means of bringing your team into a more dynamic approach which can allow you to become faster, quicker and even get ahead of the game especially during times of uncertainty.

From pharma to manufacturing to business process outsourcing, Scrum has gained more and more traction as Scrum practitioners have been able to make headway in the application of Scrum to various facets of the business world. This is something which should not be taken lightly as most organizations are in a constant search for improving their processes in such a way that they can reduce both time and cost.

That being said, it's important to take into account that Scrum is just one of the methodologies under the Agile umbrella. Thus, you have a myriad of options which you can also check out. By learning more and more about Agile, you can see just how beneficial being Agile really is.

Other Methodologies to Consider

If you are serious about going Agile, I will encourage you to check out other methodologies which can help you get the most out of your Agile mindset.

The first is Lean Manufacturing.

This methodology is focused on trimming down the fat as much as possible during manufacturing processes. Lean Manufacturing is all about reducing errors while maximizing output. Often, this is achieved through the streamlining of processes which aren't always the most efficient.

In Lean Manufacturing, the idea of "time is money" is really taken to heart.

When you become "lean," what you are essentially doing is reducing the "waste" from your processes. So, this waste can be seen as a waste of time, a waste of money and even a waste of staff. Often, businesses will hire more people than they really need. Also, they will spend a lot more time on tasks which can be done in a reduced period of time.

Now, we are not talking about firing your staff and hiring a bunch of robots to do their job.

Hardly.

What we are advocating is for having the right amount of people, within the properly designed processes, which can yield more efficient results. Consequently, efficiency will lead to better profit margins and improved revenues for companies.

Becoming lean is all about embracing an out-of-the-box approach in which you are willing to consider different angles on processes which you might be considered to have down cold. But it's when you begin thinking outside of the box that true progress is made.

Also, becoming lean is a mindset, just like Agile, in which you are looking to maximize your uptime. As you become leaner, your uptime will yield more. Hence, you will be able to take advantage of the savings obtained in term of time and resources.

A great complement to Lean Manufacturing is Six Sigma.

Six Sigma is a methodology which tracks defects and attempts to find the best ways to reduce them. So, the first step for Six Sigma practitioners is to identify the number of defects that make up the entire manufacturing process.

Six Sigma is an ideal complement to Scrum since both Six Sigma, and Scrum seeks to find the best ways to produce given the circumstances you are dealing with. In that regard, keeping a mature attitude about the reality of a company is ideal in order to make the most of any restructuring process.

Therefore, Six Sigma seeks to encourage management teams to find ways to reduce the incidence of defects. This ties into the metrics in Scrum looking to measure defects in lines of code, for instance.

As I have pointed out throughout this book, the spirit driving Scrum is continuous improvement. That is the same attitude that drives Six Sigma. As such, Six Sigma will enable you to quantify your defects in such a way that you can see where you stand, and then, make a concerted effort to improve the overall quality of your manufacturing process.

So, I would encourage you to check out these the methodology mentioned herein. They will help you find additional elements which can help you improve your overall processes in such a way that you can ensure continuous development across the lifecycle of projects, as well as, your organization's daily tasks.

As such, keeping an open mind will be just as useful to you, and your organization, as any high-priced training seminar or course you can take. Bear in mind that investing in yourself, and your team, will always be beneficial insofar as ensuring consistent results as delivered to your customers and stakeholders.

Stacking Scrum up to traditional project management methodologies

Since Scrum is relatively new on the project management scene, the more traditional project management methodologies have become increasingly scrutinized in the way they handle many of the functions associated with projecting management.

It is worth noting that the comparison that we will make in this section is not about selling Scrum as a superior means of project management. If anything, both Agile and traditional project management share many common traits.

However, it is their differences which seem to generate some controversy among advocates and practitioners of the various project management methodologies. So, I would like to point out that is it important for you to become well acquainted with the various approaches out there. When you become familiar with the myriad of the project management approaches out there, you will be able to come up with a list of items which you can confidently apply to your own project management style, as well as, helping your team rally around what you feel to be the most effective means of carrying out projects.

Since Agile, and consequently Scrum, advocates for a flat hierarchical structure, all Scrum team members have an equal say in what is done and how it is done. This is a fundamental shift from traditional project management as a traditional approached call for a hierarchical structure in which the project manager reigns supreme.

While we have clearly established this difference earlier on, it's important to consider how traditional project management is heavy on a single point of accountability. Needless to say, this may become overwhelming to that individual who must bear the responsibility for an entire project.

That being said, it is important to consider how empowerment plays a key role in providing project teams the opportunity to do things as they see fit given the fact that it is the team members who are tasked with delivering the actual value at the end of the project.

Furthermore, traditional project management considers processes as the most important elements within a project. As such, we have stated how people are more important than processes. Of course, even the most talented individuals need to have clear processes and procedures on which they can rely on. Nevertheless, when greater emphasis is placed on processes over people, then the talents of individual team members may become stifled.

Hence, it is important to foster empowerment among team members. This can be achieved by allowing team members to use their criteria, judgment, and common sense to dictate the way in which they will approach the tasks they are to complete.

This is another fundamental shift in mindset as the more individual team members are allowed to think for themselves; the lesser the burden becomes to project leaders. This is why traditional project management approaches rely so heavily on project managers. In the end, it's the project manager who bears the burden of everything that goes wrong.

Yet, if the project runs smoothly and everything comes up roses, then it's the project manager who can claim credit for everything that happened in the project. This is another fundamental shift in mindset when dealing with Scrum. If the project is a success, then the entire team takes credit for it. In a way, it's like team sports that do not rely on one player to make the difference.

Think of Rugby.

In Rugby, one player cannot be a difference-maker. One player can come to a deciding factor, but one player is not enough to win a match singlehandedly. This is where the term "Scrum" comes from. It comes from Rugby; a true team sport in every sense of the word.

This is why the collaborative nature of Scrum is at the root of the way everything is done. If Scrum practitioners truly embrace the way of this collaborative nature, then there is a good chance that the projects you embark upon will be successful.

As for traditional project management methodologies, a more segregated, differentiated division of labor is espoused. The intent behind this division of labor is to foster specialization among team members in such a way that each individual will be in their area of expertise and thereby producing results.

While this logic makes all the sense in the world, it leads to communication breakdown and even competition among the various components of the project team. So, the project manager is often a mediator among the different sections of the project. Undoubtedly, this represents additional tasks which may not be really necessary. This is not a good example of being "lean."

How to Deal with Resistance

The last topic I would like to address in this chapter is resistance.

Often, Scrum practitioners encounter resistance, especially with those folks who are unfamiliar with the principles that Agile holds true.

This resistance is mainly due to the fact that any time you ask individuals to change their ways of doing things and even approach life, you will encounter resistance. Given that this is a perfectly natural response by a human being, it is also important to consider that not everyone is open to embracing the Agile mindset.

In that sense, there are folks who would rather not be a part of Agile processes and moving away from what they know best. As such, some folks believe that advocating for the implementation of Agile methodologies is about replacing previous ideas and beliefs since Scrum is somehow much better than other methodologies

As I have stated earlier, Scrum is not "better" than other project management methodologies. It is just "better-suited" for some types of projects and industries. This is a key difference since not all projects are created equal, and certainly not all fields have the same characteristics.

This is why Scrum's cross-cutting appeal is so useful. Nevertheless, making the most of the talent and resources available is a must for all project managers. Thus, being able to communicate the benefits of Scrum to team members is a valuable first step on the road to becoming Agile.

As you traverse through the paths of becoming Agile, your team members may bring up objections as to why Agile approaches and Scrum are not the best way to go.

One of the most common issues raised by folks is the lack of a hierarchical structure.

Since hierarchy is something that is deeply rooted in the psyche of all humans, it may be hard for some folks to wrap their mind around the fact that there isn't a boss, but rather, it is a team of "bosses" that runs the project.

In addition, some folks may resist that implementing Scrum usually requires some type of retraining or courses to be taken. As such, resistance can certainly be strong especially among older folks who may not be too keen on taking courses or go through retraining efforts.

However, it is certainly worth making the most of your time to learn more about how Scrum can have a direct impact on the way that you work and how your organization can benefit from going Agile. Moreover, teams that embrace Scrum are often closer and yield better results.

As individuals begin to see the ways in which Scrum can be implemented in a positive way, the Agile mindset will begin to take hold within your organization's culture. Eventually, Scrum and Agile will become second nature to an extent whereby everything will revolve around this newfound culture.

So, I would certainly encourage you to motivate your staff to take a closer look at how Scrum and Agile can help them become a much better team. Since Agile is all about continuous improvement, then the first important concept to embrace is exactly that: continuous improvement.

As such, continuous improvement begins with individuals within your organization becoming committed to continuously improve processes, outputs, and most importantly, themselves.

Therefore, approaching continuous improvement and development should become the norm among all team members.

That being said, your organization will soon become a breeding ground for success as team members become more and more aware of the need to help each other improve. This is something that I cannot stress enough: the collaborative nature of Agile. Without it, the entire building comes crashing down.

Also, collaboration breeds trust among team members. The more team members can learn to trust each other, the more they will be willing to take on the roles and responsibilities that Agile asks of them. Moreover, when teammates really trust each other, they will develop keen instincts in which they will be able to sense everything that is going on around.

This is just like sports. When teammates truly know each other perfectly, they can produce those "no-look passes" simply because they know where their teammates are going to be. Thus, this connection among teammates can lead to producing results on a consistent basis.

Finally, I would like to underscore the importance that leadership has on a successful team. When the leadership of a team is able to provide an example of consistency and dedication, that is something which a team can rally around. While it is true that Agile does not advocate leadership in terms of being the boss, Agile does espouse a concept of leadership in which leaders must become set the standard by which team members must perform.

Consequently, the actions and attitudes of the leader will make, or break, the entire team's performance. Hence, I would greatly encourage you, if you are in a leadership position, to take your role to heart and truly become a positive influence on your teammates.

Chapter 7: Useful Resources

So, at this point, I hope that I have managed to paint a clear picture of what Agile is, and how Scrum can become an effective methodology for you and your organization. Thus, this implies embracing the Agile mindset and making changes in your overall mentality to embrace the finer points of Scrum.

However, you might be asking yourself where you can begin. This is especially true if you are not familiar with Scrum or Agile. If this is the first time you have seriously dug into the Agile mindset, then you might be eager to learn more about how you can set down the path toward embracing Agile in order to harness its full potential.

While this book was certainly a great step in the right direction, you might be looking for additional resources which can help you get your journey in Agile off to a rocking start.

So, the first place to begin is this book. Please feel free to share the knowledge you have learned here with your colleagues and teammates. You can become an agent of change by implementing this knowledge in such a way that those around you can learn more about the Agile mindset and the finer points of Scrum.

You might also be interested in holding some training sessions or meetings in which you can discuss how Agile may benefit your organization and if Agile is truly right for you and your organization. While it is true that Agile has a cross-cutting application across various fields, there may be valid reasons why Agile might not be a good fit for your organization.

Nevertheless, I am sure that the more you learn about Agile, the more you will see how many of the underlying principles in Agile, and by extension Scrum, can be applied to your organization. Of course, this is not the type of process that can happen overnight, but it is worth taking a deeper look.

By giving Scrum some serious consideration, you will be opening the door to making some interesting changes in the way business is conducted in your organization. Of course, I have no doubt that your team is currently engaged in making the most of their opportunity to deliver value, they may not be fully aware of the potential that lies in embracing a framework, such as Scrum, which can bring a certain, "logic to the madness."

However, you might not feel entirely confident about leading a Scrum-oriented process. At least not yet. Hence, you might be looking for other sources in which you can gain further insights and perspectives on implementing Scrum in your organization.

Find a Great Agile Coach

One of the best sources of knowledge and experience in the Agile world is an experienced and reputable Agile Coach. A good Agile Coach will take you and your teammates through the rigors of Agile, more specifically Scrum, and help you see how implementing Scrum can help you improve your overall processes.

Also, an Agile Coach will work with you and your team in helping you improve your overall knowledge and understanding of Agile. In doing this, the Agile Coach will help all of the members involved in this transition process become keenly aware of how Agile can be put into practice in virtually all facets of your organization's operation. Therefore, you can rest assured that you will be able to make a strong case for the implementation of Agile within your organization.

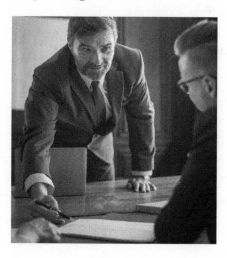

In addition, a good Agile Coach is a type of person who can hold your hand through an entire Scrum project. They can sit on the sidelines while your team takes the field. When mistakes happen, the Agile Coach will be quick to help you find the proper solution to the shortcomings your team has made. This will enable your teammates to find their rightful place within the Agile mindset in such a way that you can take full advantage of their strengths while allowing them to grow out of any limitations they may have.

Of course, an Agile Coach may not come cheap, but the overall investment would certainly be worth the time and money. Nevertheless, your organization may not be in a position to take on a full-time consultant in this capacity.

So, what other options are out there for your team to become versed in Agile and Scrum?

The Multiplier Effect

One workaround that companies and organizations use when they don't have the means to bring in full-time consultants or expensive training companies is to have a handful of staff members get trained by the experts and then multiply their knowledge and expertise.

In doing this, the organization can ensure that growth as a result of the implementation of Agile and Scrum methodologies can be born from within the company. Considering that experts and consultants have the know-how to help your organization get off the ground, it's worth mentioning that there are equally qualified individuals within your organization who can also learn from the pros and then become excellent coaches in their own right.

So, your organization might choose to send some staff off to a training course, take a class at a local college, or take an online training course. These options open the discussion to some interesting possibilities.

First, does your staff really need to take time off work in order to attend a training seminar or a class?

If you believe that it is worth giving some staff members time off to attend in-person training, then you can certainly go down that path. However, you might find that taking time off from work may not be the wisest course of action. After all, the time that staff is not working means that it is time in which tasks are not getting done.

Now, you could ask the staff to go in their free time. This may, or may not, be appealing to some. But you can be sure that if someone takes a class in their free time, it is because they are committed to learning. But this brings us to another interesting possibility: online courses.

There are several companies which offer online training courses in Agile and Scrum. They offer a number of courses and certifications which you can pursue. While not all folks are interested in becoming officially certified, holding one such certification is a great way in which you can earn some valuable credentials. Consequently, some folks are keen on becoming certified in the fields of Agile and Scrum.

Here are some of the most renowned companies in the online Agile training business:

• **Scrumstudy.com.** They offer all sorts of courses and training programs ranging from free introductory courses to full-fledged certifications. I would encourage you to check out their free courses and then look into their paid options. I believe you will find some interesting options for yourself and your teammates.

• **Scrum.org**. This company is very similar to Scrumstudy. They offer a learning path which leads to certification in addition to providing some free content to learners. This company also provides classes and training seminars which you can book in-person depending on your location.

• **Scrum Alliance**. This is one of the largest players in the Agile training world. They have a series of courses and training seminars which you can attend both online and in person. So, I would encourage you to take a closer look at how the Scrum Alliance may be able to offer you the right training solution.

- **Project management Institute** (PMI). PMI is the company behind the traditional Project Management Professional (PMP) certification. This is the most widely-respected project management certification out there. Holders of the PMP certification are heralded as pros in their field. However, PMI was a bit slow in embracing the Agile movement. Nevertheless, PMI has its own Agile training program now which is certainly worth checking out. PMI has local chapters all over the world. So, it's certainly worth giving them a look.
- **Agile Alliance**. Just like the Scrum Alliance, the Agile Alliance is focused on the broader Agile movement. So, their focus is not just on Scrum, but on all things Agile. This is a great source of information which you can check out. They have a very extensive repository of information which can check out for free. So, I would highly recommend their website for your Agile research needs.

So, there you have it. I hope you are eager to get started on the road that leads to an Agile mindset. I am sure that the information you have found in this book will help you build a convincing argument for Scrum.

However, if after reading this book you are not convinced that Agile might be right for you, then that's alright, too. As I have mentioned earlier, Agile isn't for everyone, and it certainly isn't for every organization. Nevertheless, I hope that you will give Agile and Scrum a chance. After all, you have nothing to lose but everything to gain in a new, dynamic Agile world.

Conclusion

Thank you for taking the time to read this book. If you have made it this far, it is because you are truly interested in the topic and engaged in this discussion. By taking the time to learn more about Agile and Scrum, you are opening the door to bigger and better possibilities, not just for yourself, but for your organization as well.

If you have decided to read this book as an individual who is looking to improve their skills, then you have taken a big step toward becoming an Agile expert. The next step is to learn more about Agile and Scrum. By learning more, you can decide if pursuing a formal certification is right for you. I encourage you to check out the other book in this series: *"Scrum Mastery. Agile leadership to take your team's performance from good to great."*

If you do choose to pursue a formal certification, the check out the companies which I have mentioned in the previous chapter. They have reputable training programs and can provide you with a proper path to become certified.

On the other hand, if you choose to not pursue certification, then that's great, too. I just hope that you can embrace the Agile mindset in everything you do at work and in your personal life, as well. As such, being Agile isn't just about getting stuff done at work; it's also perfectly applicable to your daily life. After all, you can search to provide your friends and family with value on a consistent basis.

If you are interested in pursuing further learning of Agile and Scrum at an institutional level, then, by all means, take the knowledge you have learned in this book and share it with your colleagues. You can hold meetings and even a training seminar in order to present your colleagues and teammates with a solid overview of what Agile is all about. Then, you can make a decision, as a team, to pursue Agile as part of your organization's philosophy.

In addition, your choice to embrace Agile as a project management methodology will certainly help provide guidance and direction to your teammates in such a way that you can ensure the success of your team in everything you do.

So, I would greatly encourage you to take the time to make the most of the opportunities you have to improve yourself and your organization's acumen by learning as much as you can about Agile. Bear in mind that Agile advocates for a continuous learning and improvement mentality. Therefore, this is a great way to live by those rules.

Finally, I would like to thank you once again for taking the time to read this book. I am well aware that there are other choices out there on this topic.

But, by reading this book, you have validated my hard work and experience.

As such, I would like to encourage you to leave a comment and be honest about what you thought of the information contained in this book. I am positive that others will find it very useful. So, if you have found this book to be interesting and informative, be sure to let others know about it!

Made in the USA
Middletown, DE
16 August 2019